AN INTRODUCTION TO Social
Research

HUBERT M. BLALOCK, JR.
The University of North Carolina

PRENTICE-HALL, INC., Englewood Cliffs, New Jersey

PRENTICE-HALL GENERAL SOCIOLOGY SERIES
Neil J. Smelser, EDITOR

© 1970 by PRENTICE-HALL, INC.
ENGLEWOOD CLIFFS, NEW JERSEY

Current printing (last digit):
10   9   8   7   6   5   4   3   2   1

C–13–496828–X
C–13–496836–0

Library of Congress catalog card number:
77–101581

Printed in the United States of America

Prentice-Hall International, Inc., London
Prentice-Hall of Australia, Pty. Ltd., Sydney
Prentice-Hall of Canada, Ltd., Toronto
Prentice-Hall of India Private Ltd., New Delhi
Prentice-Hall of Japan, Inc., Tokyo

TO DAVID W. VARLEY

Preface

My purpose in writing this short book is to attempt to explain to the introductory student and to the layman the nature of some of the basic issues that are encountered in conducting research in the social sciences. The quantitative aspects of research methodology are becoming increasingly technical, with the result that there is a growing communication gap not only between laymen and social scientists but also within the social sciences themselves. Since it would be unfortunate if we were to permit this communication gap to widen more than absolutely necessary, I believe that practicing social scientists should make every effort to explain the research process as simply as possible. In doing so, I would hope that we can provide the student and layman with a realistic perspective on the problems, limitations, and accomplishments of the social sciences. While I shall be writing primarily as a sociologist, I am convinced that most of the issues and approaches that are appropriate to my own field are also relevant, in varying degrees, to the other social sciences.

I would like to thank Charles Allyn, Desmond P. Ellis, Neil J. Smelser, James J. Teevan, Jr., and Everett K. Wilson for reading and criticising the original manuscript and Mrs. Priscilla McFarland for valuable typing services. I am especially appreciative to James H. Clark, former Prentice-Hall editor, for his active encouragement of the project.

This book is dedicated to my close friend and former colleague, David W. Varley, one of the many social scientists who have devoted their lives to undergraduate teaching.

H. M. B., JR.

Chapel Hill, N.C.

Contents

AN INTRODUCTION TO Social
Research

1

A Breakdown in Communication

After the disastrous riots of the summer of 1967, President Johnson appointed a commission to conduct a crash study of the causes of these riots and to make policy recommendations of major importance. In the aftermath of the Martin Luther King and Robert Kennedy assassinations he appointed a second blue-ribbon commission to study the causes of assassinations. These important groups contained a large majority of politicians representing both parties, plus a few black leaders, clergymen, and labor representatives. But interestingly enough, no social scientists were named, in spite of the fact that there are hundreds of social scientists who have devoted their careers to careful, objective studies of social problems. What is perhaps even more ironic is the fact that, for at least two decades, social scientists have been attempting to convince private foundations and the federal government that large-scale research must be conducted in the field of minority-group relations. They have been turned down because the subject is too controversial.

Obviously there is a breakdown of communication between social scientists and laymen when this kind of situation can occur. As a sociologist, I remember my reactions to President Johnson's appointment of the second of these committees. I couldn't conceive of anyone being so naive as to believe that a commission of politicians could conduct a study on such a complex problem as the causes of violence and assassination. To be sure, they could count noses and find out what various kinds of people *thought* were the causes, and they could recommend such things as stricter gun-control legislation and voluntary controls by the mass media. But how could they possibly conduct a valid study of the causes of violence without any knowledge of how to do research, what variables to look for, or how to control for these variables, while also being under public pressure to produce a report before the next election, riot, or assassination? [1] Do politicians really believe that this is the way to conduct research? Or is this merely another political gimmick to make the public believe that *something* is being done?

In the opinion of many social scientists, our policy makers proceed from one crisis to the next, hoping to put out each fire after it starts but without any long-range plans that would make it possible to anticipate these crises before they arise. Social scientists had for several decades pointed to the race problem, as had responsible minority leaders. But money was not available for research, much less for large-scale pilot projects or experimental programs. The same is true in the case of the population explosion. Demographers have long been aware of the problem and of the inevitable consequences unless important corrective steps are taken. But the subject of birth control is too controversial, too bound to the sacred taboo subjects of sex, religion, and family. Some day we shall probably have another presidential commission appointed to give us a crash report on the population crisis. And so it goes!

---

[1] To the credit of the appointed commission members and their staff, however, an extensive effort was made to solicit opinions from reputable social scientists as well as other citizens. The major point is that it is impossible to conduct a scientific study, involving the actual collection and analysis of data, under such pressures.

Yet obviously the fault does not lie with the politicians alone. Social scientists have not made a real effort to communicate what the research process is all about. Our journal articles are loaded with technical (and not so technical) jargon, while many of our books are best described as "popular sociology," combining a journalistic style with an almost deliberate attempt to avoid telling the reader how the research was done. In short, we have left the impression that research is either rather simple (one collects the facts and then adds them up) or not really necessary. We have not seriously challenged the nonsensical idea that there is little point in analyzing "cold" statistics when the real insights are to be obtained by seeing life as it actually is and by getting out and doing things, rather than living in the "ivory tower."

Social scientists would like to believe that the public is now prepared to listen to them more closely, to support their research, and to stop listening to those who would propose simple answers to complex problems. But I rather suspect that this hope is too optimistic. For unless one comes to appreciate the subtleties involved in the research process, he will be highly impatient with the social scientist who, in effect, says: "Wait a minute! Things aren't that simple. We really don't know that much. Our evidence is inadequate, and it would take at least ten years and a million dollars to obtain tentative answers."

The politician and businessman, the black nationalist and John Bircher, all say: "We can't wait. Our cities and colleges are burning, and we need to have immediate answers." And the social scientist replies: "You may want immediate answers, but you can't get good ones without paying a price. And that price will include sponsoring long-range, basic research in addition to applied research. Furthermore, you must anticipate the possibility that you may not like the answers you get, and you must be prepared to find that in many instances no answers can be obtained, given our present rather limited knowledge."

Since every man can think of himself as his own sociologist, psychologist, or economist, and since many social phenomena seem to have common-sense explanations, some people feel a temptation to believe that there is no real need for the social scientist. "What we need is more public housing, good jobs, and better education, not more senseless research to document the obvious!" The fact that social scientists do not see research and action programs as mutually exclusive alternatives may seem irrelevant to the activist. A sociologist would say to this argument: "Fine, by all means try out these programs. But spend a reasonable proportion of your resources on evaluation research, so that alternative programs can be compared, and so that some can be abandoned if they prove unworkable or if unanticipated outcomes result. Maintain a flexible outlook, and take advantage of the services of objective outsiders to make constructive suggestions on the basis of careful research. And in addition, devote enough funds to basic research so that general knowledge can accumulate that might (or might not) prove useful for your future programs."

The Complexity of Social Research

One of the basic difficulties that we encounter in social research, and one that has its counterpart in any attempt to find intelligent answers to pressing social problems, is the fact that in the real world a large number of variables are found to be highly interrelated. This means that their causes and effects are hard to disentangle, and there may be almost as many theories or explanations as there are people to formulate them. Both research and action planning thus become exceedingly difficult, and individual biases and ideological differences may predominate. As a result, some persons may give up the venture and fall back on the disclaimer that objective social science is impossible and that such questions must ultimately be resolved by what are essentially political means. The social scientist's answer to this thesis might run somewhat as follows:

I agree that our task is a difficult one, and we should not expect anywhere near the degree of precision that one often finds in the physical sciences. But this does not mean that we cannot make steady improvement in our theories, methodology, and data. Furthermore, we must clearly distinguish between the kinds of questions that can and cannot be answered by scientific means. While questions of what *should* be the state of affairs, what is right and wrong, who deserves what, and so forth, are questions that cannot be answered by scientific procedures, there are many questions that can be resolved by these means. In particular, the scientist can make conditional statements of the form *"if* such and such a state of affairs is desired, then the following means appear to be most efficient," or "if A then B." This kind of information is surely valuable for the policy maker, though admittedly at present we can make very few simple assertions with any degree of confidence. More realistically, our aim is to provide propositions of the form "Under conditions A, B, and C, if X were increased, then Y and Z can be expected to increase."

As a concrete illustration of the kind of complexity with which social scientists must deal, let us consider racial prejudice and discrimination in the United States. Much of the sociologist's work in the past has been devoted to documenting the extent of discrimination and prejudice of different types and to locating differences in degrees of prejudice and discrimination. For example, it has been found that Jews are generally less prejudiced than Protestants and Catholics; that residential segregation of nonwhites varies very little from city to city; that blacks are piling up in the central cities; that residential segregation of nonwhites is unrelated to their percentage in the area or to their income levels; and that industrial unions, such as the U.A.W., are much less discriminatory than craft unions. Many of these facts are now well known to the general public, though some are not obvious or explainable by common sense.

The so-called cycle of poverty has been well documented and publicized. We know that blacks (as well as other minorities, including pockets of Southern whites) tend to have low incomes, poor education, poor jobs, high unemployment rates, low motivation and achievement scores while in school, broken families, high crime and disease rates, high "alienation" scores, and a generally fatalistic and pessimistic outlook on life. We are also reasonably sure that these factors are all causally interrelated. Obviously, one needs schooling to obtain and keep a good job and a good job to earn a high income, which in turn is necessary for adequate housing. Money can help to buy one's way out of the ghetto and to provide a better education for one's children. On the other hand, living in the ghetto and being exposed to adult failures tends to perpetuate the cycle of low motivation, low achievement, high rates of school dropouts, high delinquency and crime rates, unemployment and broken homes, and so forth.

I suspect that most readers, as well as most social scientists, would agree that this rather general and vague statement is accurate as far as it goes. But whenever one finds a large number of factors that are highly related in this way, it becomes possible to select a few of one's favorites as the basic causes or explanatory variables. This leaves a wide degree of discretion and plenty of room for one's ideological biases to operate. Let me illustrate by imagining how a "sophisticated conservative" and a "sophisticated liberal" might tend to explain the cycle of poverty. We shall ignore the more naive explanations of those who would give a very simple one-factor explanation in terms, say, of the innate inferiority of blacks, the inherent defects of capitalism, or "white racism."

The argument of the sophisticated conservative might be somewhat as follows:

> Now I know that the Negro has faced discrimination and that we whites will have to change, *but* much of the fault rests with the Negro himself. After all, you cannot change human nature, nor can you expect to wipe out prejudice and discrimination by passing laws. The Negro crime rates *are* high, and many Negroes would prefer to blame everything on whites rather than trying to improve themselves. Negroes do poorly in school, even when they are given good teachers. Look at the number of fathers who leave the home and who drift. Other minorities have been able to pull themselves up by the bootstraps. After all, we are a nation of minorities, most of which have now assimilated completely. Take the case of the Jews or Japanese Americans. They have proved themselves to be acceptable middle-class groups, with strong families, good school records, and good work habits. The Negro will simply have to prove himself before he can be accepted by most whites. All of this crime and violence is merely going to cost him friends at the very time he needs them most.

The sophisticated liberal (who now replaces the word "Negro" with "black") might reply as follows:

> I'll grant you that blacks need to learn to work harder in school, to improve their family life, and reduce their crime

rate, but the fundamental reason for their relatively poor showing is the fact that whites have refused to treat them as equals. The black child's aspirations are molded by his perception of lack of opportunity. How can you expect him to finish high school when he sees black graduates unable to find work? Why should he work hard at his job when advancement is closed to him? If we are to break into the vicious cycle of poverty, blacks must be *compensated* for their handicaps in education. They must be given jobs and better housing. Welfare regulations that presently encourage the female-dominated household must give way to guaranteed incomes, family allowances, and the like. The fundamental causes of their condition are discrimination in education, jobs, and housing. They are merely reacting to this condition and have learned the hard way that they can only hope to change it by applying pressure on the white power structure.

These two interpretations—and there are, of course, many variants of each—assign different weights to the causal factors that are thought to be operative. The first stresses the Negro's responsibilities to improve himself and to take advantage of the opportunities he has. The second takes his behavior as being almost entirely dependent on his condition and on the behavior of the white majority. Undoubtedly there is some truth in both arguments. The major problem confronting the social scientist is that of deciding objectively which variables and explanations should receive the greatest weight. Can we use the canons of the scientific method, broadly interpreted, to assess their relative importance? Or will we have to rely on rhetoric, the persuasiveness of the writer, or power politics? If the latter, our opinions will also be largely determined by our own value biases and self-interest. If the former, there is at least a reasonable chance that cooler heads will prevail.

Certain methodological difficulties make it difficult to provide really definitive answers to many important questions that might be asked of the social scientist. Some of these difficulties are shared by all the sciences, physical as well as social, and stem from limitations inherent to the scientific method. Some are purely technical methodological problems that have not yet been satisfactorily resolved. Others can be tackled, but we merely lack the data, either because no one has thought to study the question or because he was prevented from doing so owing to its controversial nature.

In the remainder of this book I shall attempt to state what I see as the major methodological problems and approaches that are characteristic of my own discipline, sociology, and which to varying degrees are also characteristic of the other social sciences, particularly political science, psychology, economics, and anthropology. We can begin by examining the nature of the experimental method, which is usually taken as the ideal form of scientific research. While the experimental model often cannot be utilized in many kinds of social research, it provides a useful basis of comparison with nonexperimental research, which is far more common in the social sciences.

A Note to the Student

In the remainder of this book I shall be primarily concerned with the task of attempting to explain certain major aspects of the research process in relatively simple terms. Students, especially, are prone to ask of every topic they study, "What is its relevance to major social problems? How will a knowledge of this subject help me to understand and control my social environment?" In general terms, I believe a very simple answer can be given to this question. Well established scientific principles based on sound research are usually a *necessary* condition for intelligent social action, but they are not in themselves sufficient. That is, even though we possess the necessary knowledge, this is no guarantee that we will be either able or willing to act on the basis of this knowledge. But without the knowledge, we will find it necessary to continue using the kinds of trial and error methods that have thus far proved highly inefficient and socially costly.

The scientist, as scientist, is not directly concerned with the applications to which his findings or theories are relevant, although as a citizen he may be very much interested in these applications. When playing the role of scientist he must strive toward objectivity, whereas as a citizen he must inevitably take a stand, if only to "stand aside" while others apply his knowledge. This dual role is never easy to play. If the scientist becomes an extreme partisan he may find that he loses his objectivity and his ability to analyze data impartially. But if he becomes completely unconcerned as to how knowledge is applied, and if he takes an extreme "science for science's own sake" position, he may become willing to sell his services to the highest bidder. So-called "establishment" social scientists have recently been accused by New Left students of having become handmaidens of the power elite who purportedly are using studies of underprivileged groups for the purpose of controlling their behavior. While charges such as these are highly exaggerated, there is always enough truth to them that they must be taken seriously.

As a science matures to the point where its findings become increasingly useful to the sponsoring agency, the responsibilities of the scientist as citizen become correspondingly greater. No science can afford to play a completely passive role in relation to potential applications of knowledge. Yet it cannot be the primary business of the scientist, when he is acting as a scientist, to be overly concerned with these applications. Thus there is an inherent strain in the role of the scientist-citizen that cannot be denied. In this short book, however, we cannot devote our attention to this important subject, which has become especially crucial in these troubled times.[2]

To those students who would wish to study society with the full recognition that resolutions to social problems will not be simple or immediate and who are willing to devote the necessary time to the task, this brief introduction to research methods should be sufficient to indicate the magnitude of the job that lies ahead. The emphasis in the remaining chapters will be on the complexities one can expect to encounter in the research process. It is often much easier to point to difficulties than it is to overcome them, since the latter requires considerably more technical knowledge and resources. But if these difficulties are underestimated or ignored, we shall merely have to pay the price at some later time. If one wishes to undertake serious research in the social sciences, he should begin the task with his eyes wide open.

---

[2] A book that was written thirty years ago on this subject is still relevant in many respects today. See Robert S. Lynd, *Knowledge for What?* (Princeton, N.J.: Princeton University Press, 1939).

2

Some Principles of Experimental Design

My purpose in this chapter is to present enough of the basic ideas of experimental designs for the reader to see how it is possible to build and elaborate on very elementary principles of design to the point where reasonably complex studies and analyses can be made. Readers will naturally differ with respect to degree of interest and background in the subject. Since my main objective is to communicate, rather than to confuse or overwhelm, I shall confine the discussion to nontechnical matters, though I hope that I will at the same time be able to convey the fact that the subject of experimental design is a complex one that cannot be mastered without considerable background in statistics.

Let us begin with a very simple intuitive idea of the ideal experiment. There will be one or more variables whose behavior we wish to understand or control. We shall refer to such variables as "dependent" variables. We make the fundamental assumption that the values of these variables are influenced by another set of variables taken to be possible causes of the behavior of these dependent variables. We refer to these causally prior variables as "independent" variables, recognizing that the real world may be much more complex than this simple idealization would seem to imply.

We then set out to isolate and infer the effects of one or more independent variables on the dependent variables. To simplify further, let us assume for the time being that we are dealing with a single dependent variable (say, aggression toward blacks) and that we wish to infer the effects of a single independent variable (say, degree of frustration). Common sense would suggest that if it were possible to hold constant all of the remaining causes of the dependent variable, and if we could then vary the single remaining independent variable systematically and observe what happened to the dependent variable, we should be able to infer the effects of the independent variable X (here, frustration) on the dependent variable Y (here, aggression). In particular, for each level of X we ought to be able to associate some level of Y, as indicated in Figure 1.

Several things might be noted from this figure. First, not all the points fit exactly on a smooth curve. In the ideal, if all disturbing factors had been held constant, we might expect that all points would lie exactly on the curve. But why? Why should they be any more likely to fall on a smooth curve than

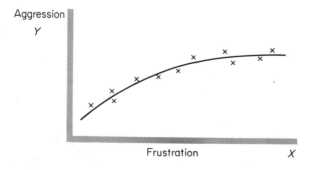

Figure 1

on an irregular one? Why should nature or reality conform to our aesthetic sense of what is proper? In fact it may not, but it is certainly convenient to believe that it does, for then we can describe the relationship by a simple mathematical formula, pretending that deviations are either of trivial importance or explainable in terms of measurement error.[1] We see the necessity and desirability of oversimplifying reality so as to economize our thought processes. This method is not peculiar to the social sciences. It holds true for all abstraction and generalization, but it has been used most systematically in the physical sciences.

The second thing we notice from Figure 1 is that the curve relating X to Y is not necessarily a straight line. In this particular case, as X increases Y increases but at a decreasing rate. Put another way, at high levels of frustration a given increase in X does not produce a very big change in aggression Y—nowhere near as large a change in Y as would occur when X is small. The general point is that a mathematical curve is much more precise than is the simple statement: "The greater the frustration, the greater the aggression." The experimenter might have begun with a crude verbal hypothesis to this effect, and his experimental result might not only have confirmed his hunch but refined it as well.

Unfortunately, there is an extremely important assumption that has thus far been ignored. How can one possibly know whether all remaining causes of aggression have been controlled? Clearly, there can be no conceivable way to test this assumption, since a skeptic can always point to some uncontrolled variable that might be a possible cause. Since it is manifestly impossible to list all causes or influences that might disturb a relationship, it will obviously be impossible to test this assumption. Philosophers have known all this for a long time, and the notions of cause and effect have become disreputable as a result. Nevertheless, this fact has not prevented

---

[1] Of course there may also be sound theoretical reasons for expecting smooth curves in many instances. Perhaps because humans learn to react in terms of others' expectations, the curves representing their responses could be expected to be smooth rather than jagged.

the practicing scientist from using the terms—or their equivalents—nor has it prevented him from conducting experiments and making inferences on the basis of their results. It has simply made him more cautious and a bit more humble.

How can one get around this difficulty, if only for practical purposes? One point we might note is the following common result. If there are in fact numerous disturbing factors, not all acting in concert, then we will generally find a distribution of results something like that of Figure 2, where the scores are scattered fairly widely about the smooth curve that has been drawn through them. The situation is now much more ambiguous. In the first place, if there is a wide scattering of points, it will be much more difficult to approximate them with any single smooth curve, and there will be numerous curves that succeed almost equivalently well in fitting the data. Some criterion of what one means by a "best fit" will be necessary, and curve-fitting by simple inspection will have to be replaced by more rigorous methods that can be replicated by all observers.

Secondly, with a good deal of scatter there is always the

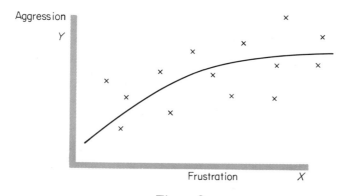

Figure 2

strong chance that one or two uncontrolled variables are distorting the relationship between X and Y. Perhaps there is no causal connection between frustration X and aggression Y. Maybe a third variable Z is a common cause of both X and Y so that, unless it is controlled, there will appear to be a causal relationship between them when in fact there is none. This simple situation can be diagramed as follows:

In such a case we call the relationship between X and Y "spurious." It is there in the data, but we would be incorrect if we were to infer from these data that it is frustration that is producing the aggression. X and Y are associated or correlated, and we could in fact predict or estimate the one from the other, but there is no causal connection of practical or theoretical significance. For example, if we were to base a policy decision on this association, hoping to reduce aggression Y by reducing frustration, we would be disappointed. Instead, we should have manipulated Z, one of the true causes of Y. Of course, the problem is that we might not be aware of the existence of Z and its influence on Y. The greater the scatter of points, the more likely we are to suspect the presence of such disturbing influences. But the absence of scatter is not sufficient to disprove the presence of other factors. Even with a perfect fit of the data to the curve, it is always possible that, had some third factor been held constant, the original relationship might have been altered considerably.

We have identified two sorts of error in this example, truly random scatter and systematic distortions produced by uncontrolled variables such as Z. In most practical examples there will be some errors of each type, but unfortunately we will not be in a position to evaluate their relative magnitudes. Our best bet is to eliminate possible sources of error by careful design. But how can this be accomplished in the presence of very large numbers of disturbing factors, most of which will be unknown? R. A. Fisher, the noted biologist and one of the founders of modern statistics, has emphasized that many sources of systematic error can be handled by the process of randomization, through which subjects are assigned to "treatments" or experimental manipulations purely by chance.[2] Let us illustrate this process in terms of our frustration example.

Suppose the experimenter decides that he will use two levels of frustration (moderate and high) plus a control group that will be treated just like the others, except that it will not receive any (deliberately induced) frustration. One example of such a study in a rather natural setting took place at a boys' summer camp at which one group of boys was made to take an impossible test that forced them to miss bank night at the movies, whereas a control group did not undergo this experience.[3] Both groups were given identical opportunities before and after the experience to express prejudice toward minorities. The objective was to see if the boys who had been frustrated expressed a significant change in their prejudice levels as compared with the control group, as in fact they did.

Obviously there are a number of personality factors that could also account for the difference. Some boys might not really have cared about bank night and might have enjoyed the tests. Some might have had greater frustration tolerance than others. Many might be expected to express their hostility by aggressing against their counselors or fellow campers rather than against minorities. Some might have turned their aggression inward out of force of habit.

Had the boys been able to decide which group they were to enter, perhaps by volunteering to take the tests, then there would be no assurance that personality characteristics were similarly distributed in the two groups. Perhaps those most

[2] Fisher's classic work on the subject became the cornerstone for much of modern statistical inference. See R. A. Fisher, *The Design of Experiments* (Edinburgh: Oliver & Boyd, 1937).

[3] See N. E. Miller and R. Bugelski, "Minor Studies in Aggression: the Influence of Frustrations Imposed by the In-group on Attitudes Expressed Toward Out-groups," *Journal of Psychology*, 25 (1948), 437–42.

prone to minority aggression would volunteer to be in the experimental group, and this fact, rather than the frustration experienced, might account for the difference in responses. One way to check on this indirectly is to measure both groups before the experience; but, as we shall see, such a tactic might lead to additional complications. The intuitively obvious answer is to flip a coin to decide which boys go into the experimental group. This is a simple illustration of what Fisher meant by randomization.

Returning to our three-group example, we might consider the following somewhat more complicated procedure. Suppose we fully expect that intelligence (as measured by I.Q. scores) and age are both likely to affect the outcomes, along with numerous unmeasured personality traits. Individuals may be placed in trios by matching them with respect to age and I.Q. to whatever degree of precision is desirable. One triplet might contain persons aged 18 with I.Q.'s between 110 and 120; a second might consist of three 25-year-olds with I.Q.'s of 140 or above. Obviously, it will be difficult and impractical to match very many variables at once. There won't be enough trios with the right combinations of characteristics, and many potential subjects will have to be omitted. But having matched on age and I.Q., we can be assured that any differences we may find among the three groups cannot be due to these particular variables. We then use some random device, such as the toss of a die, to decide which member of each trio goes into the control group, which into the group with moderate frustration, and which into the remaining group. We do not let them volunteer, nor do we rely on our own personal judgment or any other nonrandom factors.

What does randomization do exactly? It does not place a rigid control over any factor. If there turn out to be personality differences among the three groups, they will continue to operate and to disturb the final results. Thus they are not being controlled in the strict sense of being the same for all three groups (as age and I.Q. would be in this example). In effect, we rely on the laws of probability to produce similar distributions of all factors that the individuals carried with them into the experiment. This is not the place to discuss probability theory, but the general idea should be familiar to most readers. If each group is large enough, we would expect that average levels of frustration tolerance, initial prejudice, enjoyment of bank night, and so forth will be approximately the same in all three groups. This statement is based on the same intuition and experience that enables one to predict that the average coin will come up heads about half the time in the long run, that the combination of 7 for two dice is more likely than any other sum, and that bridge hands tend to equalize in the long run. The major advantage of randomization is that it takes care of numerous factors, all at once, without our having to know what they are.

Why bother with matching on age and I.Q. then? Wouldn't randomization take care of them too? It would, but we must always remember that chance may play tricks on us and that, where we know or strongly suspect that one or two variables are likely to be important, it is better to keep them under rigid control if feasible. We do this with as many variables as possible and then randomize the rest. In effect, when we resort to randomization we admit that we have been unable to hold all causal variables strictly constant, and therefore we will have scatter or unexplained variation. The purpose of randomization is to make this scatter approximately random rather than systematically related to the two variables whose relationship we are studying. In this particular example, we want to make the effects of numerous personality factors be unrelated to the experimental variable, the amount of frustration.

Randomization is thus a much more efficient device than holding all variables constant, even where they are known. Many factors will be of only minor importance individually, though their aggregate effect may be pronounced. It would be ridiculous to attempt to measure them all carefully and keep them rigidly under control when randomization can in effect enable the investigator to assume that their effects have safely been canceled out. Furthermore, the statistician can calculate exact probabilities enabling one to pin down the chances of distortions being greater than a given magnitude. By increasing the sample size and modifying the design, the scientist can gain almost any degree of precision he desires, though in general the more precision he wants the larger his sample must be.

Multiple Experimental Variables

It has been pointed out that randomization increases efficiency of design. There are additional ways to increase efficiency in instances where the investigator is interested in studying the effects of more than one experimental variable at once. In most studies there will be at least two or three variables or factors that may combine in peculiar ways. For example, in agricultural experiments it is frequently desirable to try out different combinations of soil types, fertilizers, and seed types. Perhaps a given fertilizer works best in combination with a particular soil type. Or two fertilizers may work equally well on certain types of plants but not others. In such instances, if one were to look singly at the fertilizer types, and then hold fertilizer constant and vary the soil type, and then compare different kinds of seeds, he might overlook the peculiar combinations of joint effects or what are called "interactions" in the statistical literature. Quite apart from this, he would find it necessary to conduct a large number of different experiments where one might have sufficed.

As soon as one allows for combinations of experimental variables, the statistical analysis can become rather complicated. Suffice it to say that techniques have been worked out for estimating each of the so-called "main effects" (average effects) of the separate experimental variables, plus the "interaction" effects of various combinations over and above the main effects. There will also be random variation, so that probability statements can be made about the magnitude of possible effects of variables that have not been perfectly controlled in the randomization process. Let us illustrate in terms of a somewhat different example.

Suppose a social scientist is attempting to study aggression among lower-class children by designing an experiment in a school setting in which the teacher is given different sets of instructions as to how to deal with aggressive behavior. Obviously, the teacher herself is a factor, since not all teachers will use the same approaches or be equally effective. From the standpoint of the investigator, the teacher is a "nuisance" factor with real effects that he would hope could be ignored. But some teachers may work best with one technique, whereas others may be more effective with a second. This would be an example of interaction, as discussed above. The investigator might like to be able to recommend that method B is superior to methods A and C for all teachers, but this might be unrealistic. If he finds that some teachers are relatively more effective with one method than another, he has an additional task. He must find out why this should be the case. Perhaps it is a matter of experience, or the age of the teacher, or her teacher training, or some personality factor. If so, he would have to qualify his generalization by recommending method B only for certain kinds of teachers.

Perhaps the investigator also suspects that the size of the class has some bearing on the effectiveness of the method. Method A may work best for small classes but may require too intensive control for a larger class. Suppose, then, that there are three experimental variables to be studied together: the method for controlling aggression, the teacher, and the class size.[4] If these were studied naturally, as they might occur without manipulation in an actual school setting, one might

---

[4] Of course the teacher is not a "variable" in any strict sense of the term. When we speak about the "teacher variable" we are in effect admitting our ignorance as to what produces differences among teachers. If we find such differences, our next step is to construct sets of variables (e.g., teacher's age, experience, personality traits) that can account for these differences.

find the following kind of situation, which is purely hypothetical. Mrs. Jones, who has been teaching for thirty years and who thoroughly dislikes aggressive children, has in effect been using method A. Since she has earned seniority, she has been given relatively small classes. Mrs. Smith and Mrs. Brown, both new, prefer method C, and there is no one using method B. Mrs. Smith, though young, is intolerant of aggressive children, whereas Mrs. Brown is not. They are good friends and discuss their techniques and problems frequently. Mrs. Brown happens to have a much larger class than Mrs. Smith because of a last-minute resignation of one of the teachers.

In natural settings such as this, one ordinarily expects to find the independent variables of interest mixed together or highly interrelated. Teachers who prefer method A may always teach the larger classes, and so forth. This confounding of independent or causal variables is one of the basic reasons why we have difficulties in nonexperimental research. In this illustration we could not separate the teacher effect from the method or size effect. In our discrimination example it is difficult to separate the effects of education, employment, income, housing, and broken homes, all of which tend to be highly interrelated.

The basic advantage of the experimental design, in addition to the possibility of randomization, is that one may manipulate the situation so that all of the independent or causal variables are made to be unrelated to each other in the experiment. For example, the investigator may decide to use three teaching methods, four different teachers, and two class sizes (say 15 and 30 students). The essential feature of experimental designs is in their symmetry with respect to numbers of replications, which makes it possible to separate the various main effects and interaction effects. In this example each technique might be tried the same number of times for both class sizes and by all four teachers. Each teacher, in turn, will have equal numbers of classes of the two different sizes. One possible combination might be as follows:

Class Size	Teacher Number			
	1	2	3	4
Small	A	A	A	A
	A	A	A	A
	B	B	B	B
	B	B	B	B
	C	C	C	C
	C	C	C	C
Large	A	A	A	A
	A	A	A	A
	B	B	B	B
	B	B	B	B
	C	C	C	C
	C	C	C	C

We see that each teacher uses method A four times, twice each with small and large classes. The same is true for methods B and C. Looking at it another way, there are no systematic teacher or class-size differences among the three methods. If the mean aggression score for the three methods is found to differ more than one would expect by chance, given the possibility of random disturbances, then this cannot be due to systematic teacher or size differences. Similarly, if aggression is more pronounced in large classes than small ones, this cannot be due to teacher or method effects. By comparing the three sets of means (one for differences among teachers, a second for differences among methods, and the third for the sizes), one can obtain estimates of the various main effects. These will tell us which of the three variables is most important, on the average. Perhaps there is very little difference between the two class sizes.

Although the detailed reasoning is too complex to be treated here, one can also obtain estimates of the peculiar combination effects, or interactions. All teachers but the first might work best with method B. But the difference between B and C might be very unimportant in the larger classes, whereas in the smaller ones B might be definitely superior. If it were suspected that teacher 1, who is more effective with method A, is really more typical of teachers than any of the remainder, then a follow-up experiment might be made in order to learn more about teacher differences. In this second experiment a larger number of teachers might be used at the expense of dropping, say, method *C*. On the other hand, if class size proved to be more important than teacher differences, a second experiment might involve a larger number of size and method combinations.

An element of randomization should also enter the experiment. If the order in which a teacher taught her classes were expected to make a difference, this order might be systematically varied, perhaps by having teacher 1 teach in the order *ABCABC*, whereas teacher 2 used the order *BCABCA*, and so forth. If this could not be done efficiently, then the order could be randomly selected. Most important, the students should be assigned to the classes randomly, so that all of the really aggressive children were not placed together in the same classroom, with rather disastrous "interaction" effects of a different kind.

The elements of randomization and symmetry are of basic importance in all experimental designs. The remaining details can be modified according to one's interests, cost factors, and the like. For example, if one were willing to assume that no interactions would be present, and that the main effects were the only ones of interest, then it would be possible to get by with many fewer classes by using what is called a "Latin-Square" design in which the number of teachers, methods, and sizes are all the same. For example, suppose one used three teachers and three sizes (large, medium, and small) along with the three methods. The design might be as follows:

| | Teacher Number | | |
Class Size	1	2	3
Small	A	B	C
Medium	B	C	A
Large	C	A	B

In this design we see that each method is used three times, once by each teacher and once with each class size. But each method is not used with each *combination* of teacher and size, as was true for the previous design. Therefore if there are peculiar teacher-size interactions (e.g., teacher 1 works best with large classes, teacher 2 with medium ones, and teacher 3 with small ones), this kind of interaction effect will be confounded with the main effects of method (e.g., method C will look better than the others merely because of the teacher-size interaction). Thus, although this Latin-Square design enables the experimenter to separate out all three main effects with many fewer replications (and therefore less cost), it requires the assumption that all interactions are zero.

The general principle illustrated by this comparison of designs is that one must always make decisions that involve swapping efficiency (and cost) for ability to test assumptions. Some untestable assumptions must always be made in any piece of scientific research. The major dilemma one faces is how many he can afford to make, as compared with the price of a more complex design that might test more of these assumptions and provide more information.

Assumptions About the Manipulations

Thus far we have assumed that randomization can take care of disturbing factors, as long as each group contains a large enough number of cases for random errors to cancel each other out, so to speak. (Just how large is "large enough" is a technical question that requires a knowledge of statistical inference.) This kind of assumption may be realistic in the case of agricultural experiments on wheat yields, where the wheat does not generally react to the fact that it is being experimented on.[5] But what about human beings? The mere fact

---

[5] This distinction between reactions that occur when human beings are being measured and those that, presumably, do not occur with plants or objects in the physical environment should not be overdrawn. There are many instances in the physical sciences where the process of measurement may disturb the behavior of the object being measured.

that they know they are in an experiment, or that the setting is somewhat strange, may influence their behavior. Another common problem is that the experimenter may think that he is manipulating only one variable, such as frustration, whereas actually he may be manipulating several at once, and these unknown variables may actually be the ones that are producing the differences.

This problem can be illustrated in terms of a classic study conducted during the depression of the 1930's, before social scientists had become sensitized to this sort of difficulty.[6] The study involved the productivity of workers making electrical equipment in the Hawthorne Electrical Company, and the phenomenon the investigators discovered has been dubbed the "Hawthorne Effect." In brief, a group of girls was set apart and their work productivity measured after a series of changes involving improved lighting, longer rest pauses, and better incentive plans. Each time a change was made their productivity increased, leaving the impression that each change was one for the better. As a final check, the experimenters returned to the original unfavorable conditions of poor lighting, no rest pauses, and no incentive system. Productivity still went up, contrary to all expectations. What had happened? The obvious explanation was that the motivation of the girls had been improving all along, not because of the specific changes but because they were flattered at having been singled out and given extra attention by management. They were important, for the first time in their occupational histories.

This kind of experimentation would nowadays seem extremely naive, and it has led many skeptics to claim that experiments with human subjects will inevitably be misleading. There is something artificial about the experimental setting. How do we know that introductory psychology students being paid for volunteering in experiments will really act normally or like people who are very different from themselves? These are important problems, to which social scientists have

[6] This study and other similar ones are reported in detail in F. J. Roethlisberger and W. J. Dickson, *Management and the Worker* (Cambridge, Mass.: Harvard University Press, 1939).

given considerable thought. While these difficulties cannot be completely overcome, there have been a number of different approaches aimed at getting around the most serious kinds of objections.

Many investigators will go to great lengths to make the experimental setting seem natural. For example, if the above hypothetical experiment on school children were carried out in their own schools, with their normal teachers, and with no word to the parents that anything unusual was going on, the chances would seem rather remote that the children would behave unnaturally. Instead of a small group meeting in a laboratory setting, an experiment might be conducted in a more natural place: someone's home, a club room, and so forth. Measurements might appear in the form of games, in the case of children, or perhaps as part of research being conducted by someone completely unconnected with the supposed purposes of the study. And if the fact of measurement could not be hidden, the true purpose of the study might be disguised by various means. One very effective device is to plant someone in the group, with the instructions that he is to act in a given way regardless of the outcome, so that it becomes possible to standardize events without their seeming to be unnatural.

Procedures such as these create certain inherent dilemmas. One dilemma that must always be resolved is the necessity of compromising between the need for a natural setting, one that will not seem artificial or give away the purpose of the study, and a more controlled setting that is standard across all groups. For example, there might be twenty groups receiving various combinations of treatments, as in our previous example. If the settings were in private homes, or in other ways were kept as natural as possible, there might be all kinds of interruptions and other kinds of differences that could make the results noncomparable. Ideally, one would want to hold most of these kinds of disturbances constant, since they cannot be randomized according to strict procedures (though one might hope that their effects canceled each other out).

A second kind of dilemma that nearly always arises involves ethical questions. Certainly the subject is to be protected from harmful experiments or any experiments that would turn friend against friend, hurt someone's ego by providing him with false information about his abilities, or put him in extremely uncomfortable positions during the course of the experiment. In many instances these kinds of moral dilemmas can be resolved by informing the subjects after the experiment has been finished as to what its true purposes were. But on a college campus, where word quickly gets around about "cute" experiments, this kind of feedback about the purposes of the study could be disastrous. Frequently the true purposes must be disguised, but any ego-threatening experiences may have to be set straight. For example, if a student subject has been fed the false information that his coworkers did much better than he did on an intelligence test, he may be told at the end of the study that a mistake had been made and that actually he had done very well.

An equally serious problem is that of preventing exploitation in reverse, namely preventing subjects from defeating the purpose of the study by not taking it seriously and even by trying to outguess the experimenter. Here it is essential to find ways of motivating the subject by making the proper appeal. In some cases he is paid. If he is playing a competitive game, for example, he may be rewarded according to his performance. In other cases an appeal may be made to his intellectual curiosity or to the advancement of science. He may be given partial course credit for participation. In addition, a good deal of effort must be made to make the experiment an interesting one that ego-involves the participants so that they forget they are in an experiment and begin to act naturally after a few practice trials. It is the task of methodologists—those who study the social scientists' research procedures—to attempt evaluation studies to see which kinds of appeals seem most effective. In other words, there are social scientists who conduct experiments on experiments!

In addition to these kinds of complications, there is also the possibility that the initial measurements made on both the control and experimental groups may themselves affect the outcomes. For example, if boys are given an initial prejudice test designed to see whether or not the control and experimental groups have been well matched prior to the experiment, some of them may become sensitized as to the purpose of the experiment. When the test is later repeated, they may remember their responses and attempt to appear consistent. Or their interest in the dependent variable (in this case, prejudice) may be aroused to the point where they may be influenced by factors other than the experimental variable.

The main effects of the premeasure itself may be canceled out by subtracting the scores of the control and experimental groups. For example, suppose the following figures represented mean scores on the before and after measurements of the control and experimental groups:

| | Group Receiving: | | |
	No Frustration	Moderate Frustration	High Frustration
Before	50	46	43
After	55	54	66

It could be reasoned that since the mean score for the control group, without any frustration, increased by five points from 50 to 55, we could expect that the remaining two groups might be similarly affected by whatever induced this change in the control group. Perhaps this change was due to the premeasurement or to uncontrolled events of which the experimenter was unaware. There may have been so-called "maturational effects" such as fatigue, hunger, or (in more long-range experiments) a learning experience.

We note an increase from 46 to 54 in the second group. This represents a change of eight points, five of which might be attributed to the same effects of premeasurement or uncontrolled events operating on the control group. Therefore it might be assumed that the frustration experience itself had only the small impact of increasing the average score by a net amount of three units. On the other hand, in the third group the total change is twenty-three points, eighteen of which might be attributed to the effects of high frustration. The investigator might infer that whereas moderate frustration does not have much effect on aggression (of this type), a larger amount has a considerable impact.

But the situation is not so simple if there is an interaction effect between the premeasurement or uncontrolled factors and the experimental variable. Suppose the premeasurement sensitizes boys who receive the frustrating experience but not those who are in the control group. Or suppose uncontrolled events plus the experimental variable produce unusual effects that would not be obtained under other circumstances. One way to study possible interaction of premeasurement effects with those of the experimental variable is to introduce two additional groups that have not been premeasured, one of which is also exposed to the experimental variable whereas the other is not.[7] Provided that randomization can be counted on to equalize the four groups, it can be shown that interactions involving the premeasurement can be estimated by means of this four-group design. But since it will be manifestly impossible to expose some groups to uncontrolled events while others are not, interactions between these uncontrolled events and the experimental variable will always be confounded with the main effects of the experimental variable.

This is a fundamental difficulty that can be avoided only by controlling the uncontrolled events as carefully as possible! But the more carefully they are controlled, the less "natural" the experimental setting often becomes and the more difficult it is to generalize from experimental findings to the real world, where uncontrolled events occur with such regularity that they

[7] A very readable discussion of these basic designs is given in Claire Selltiz, Marie Jahoda, Morton Deutsch, and S. W. Cook, *Research Methods in Social Relations* (New York: Holt, Rinehart & Winston, 1959).

become part of the scene of human events. For this reason, many social scientists are skeptical that rigid experimental designs can be applied to any but the simplest kinds of human affairs.

Practical Implications

For the most part, experimental research has been conducted by psychologists working with animals or rather basic human responses, such as perception or simple learning. Social psychologists have also adapted experimental methods to small groups in laboratory settings. These studies have the advantage of being relatively inexpensive and capable of being conducted over relatively brief periods of time. In spite of the difficulties with experimental research—which are certainly no more formidable than is the case for nonexperimental alternatives— these small-group studies have provided numerous theoretical insights for the social scientist.

There has also recently developed an interest in applying experimental methods to much larger-scale projects involving entire communities. For example, a very ambitious experiment on alternative fertility and family-planning programs has been conducted in Taiwan, with the assistance of sociologists from the University of Michigan.[8] One encounters certain practical difficulties in these large-scale projects in addition to those already mentioned. Often political decisions determine which communities receive the experimental programs and which do not. This permits the kind of self-selection that randomization has been designed to eliminate. For example, if only the communities with the right kind of leadership receive the experimental treatment, and if these communities are found to change more rapidly than the control communities, the difference may be due to leadership differences rather than to the program itself.

[8] See Bernard Berelson and Ronald Freedman, "A Study in Fertility Control," *Scientific American*, 210 (May 1964), 3–11.

The only way to get around this sort of political difficulty is to convince the layman that experiments must be conducted according to sound principles if the results are to be conclusive. This means, of course, that if action projects are to be adequately evaluated, social scientists must be brought into the decision-making process at the beginning stages, not after the programs are already in progress. This all seems like common sense once one begins to grasp even the most elementary principles of experimental design, but it still seems too poorly understood by those who are responsible for making the basic decisions. Perhaps this is because a really careful design would show that the experimental program is not having any effect. In the short run, such knowledge might be harmful to its initiators, but in the long run I do not see how rational decisions can be based on any other procedure.

As a final remark, I would like to emphasize a general point that should be readily apparent from this very brief survey of experimental designs. The research process always consists of a series of compromises. At each point where an important decision must be made there must be a judgment as to whether a given piece of data, or an untested assumption, is worth the extra expense or sacrifice that will be necessary in order to obtain the required information. If an investigator decides in favor of one variable or research design, he is forced to neglect another.

Ideally these decisions should be based on prior knowledge obtained through cumulative research findings. The less advanced the field, and the less certain this knowledge, the less plausible will be the assumptions one is required to make. But *all* research involves certain untested assumptions, frustrating as this fact may be to both scientist and layman alike. It is important for both to realize what assumptions are being made at each stage of the research process. Such understanding requires a basic minimum knowledge of research design. It also requires that one be tolerant of the ambiguities and qualifications of findings with which all social scientists have learned to deal.

3

Exploratory and Descriptive Studies

Our discussion of experimental designs has presupposed not only that the investigator is actually in a position, practically speaking, to carry out an experiment but that he also knows quite a bit about the nature of the phenomena he is investigating. It has been suggested that a well designed experiment might involve the simultaneous manipulation of perhaps three or four variables, combined with rigid controls (as through matching) on perhaps two or three more, and with randomization handling a good many of the remainder. But what if there appear to be a much larger number of potential variables of interest, with little previous knowledge or theory that would tell one where to begin? In these kinds of situations, which are perhaps the most common ones in many areas of anthropology, political science, and sociology, a much more flexible and exploratory approach will be needed. In the present chapter we shall consider two types of more exploratory studies that are characterized by two very different kinds of data-collection techniques. The first is that of participant observation; and the second, that of the descriptive sample survey.

When a writer speaks about the variables he is using, the reader may not realize that a tremendous amount of preliminary work may have gone into the construction of the measure. We shall postpone a more general consideration of measurement until Chapter 5, but it is advisable to discuss very briefly the fact that there may be different levels at which measurement, in the generic sense, may be attained. This will then lead directly to a consideration of participant observation as an exploratory approach to the formulation of new concepts, measures, and preliminary hypotheses.

Levels of Measurement

NOMINAL SCALES

On the crudest and simplest level, classification may be thought of as measurement. If one can classify individuals into mutually exclusive and exhausive categories, then it becomes possible to count cases and to see the degree to which one category predicts to another. For example, if adults can be classified as "Protestants," "Catholics," "Jews," and "Others," and also as "Republicans," "Democrats," "Independents," and "Others," they can then be cross-tabulated as follows:

	Protestants	*Catholics*	*Jews*	*Others*	*Total*
Republicans	500	100	50	30	680
Democrats	300	300	200	40	840
Independents	100	80	100	20	300
Others	100	20	50	10	180
Total	1000	500	400	100	2000

There is no ordering necessarily implied in such classifications. One could interchange two columns or rows without making any difference. Sometimes these groupings may be used in such a way as to imply an ordering, however, as for example if political party were taken as an indicator of political liberalism. In such an instance, one might wish to insert the Independents between the Republicans and Democrats, leaving the "Other" category as a residual grouping including communists, socialists, vegetarians, and persons who are completely nonpolitical. These simple classifications are often referred to as "nominal scales," deriving from the fact that we have simply given a *name* to the category without implying anything else.

There are, of course, many ways that individuals may be categorized, but only a few of these will be practically or theoretically useful. In the above example we have categorized persons by religious denomination because we believe that denomination will be related to some other basis for classification, such as political preference. If this in fact turns out to be the case, as is true in the above table, then we may make statements to the effect that Protestants are more likely to be Republicans than are either Catholics or Jews. This may be a research finding, or it may be predicted in advance of data collection and be tested as an hypothesis. In a preliminary study, such as the kinds we are about to discuss, an investigator may be left with a definite impression that relatively more people of one kind (e.g., Protestants) are also likely to be something else (e.g., Republicans), but he may not have had the opportunity to do the actual counting. In a descriptive survey, on the other hand, the actual numerical data may have been obtained and the findings set forth in terms of tables of the above form.

ORDINAL SCALES

People are often relatively easy to categorize, and in fact they place each other into categories all the time. Mr. Jones may be an accountant, married, a Presbyterian, a Moose, a grandfather, may live on a farm, and so forth. These are manifest characteristics, so to speak. A much more difficult task, however, is that of finding useful ways of *ordering* these classes according to meaningful criteria. For example, most Americans freely admit that occupations can be roughly ranked according to their prestige, though there may be minor disagreements and certain kinds of occupations (e.g., farming) that are difficult to place. Therefore a person may be given an occupational prestige score that places him on a continuum from high to low (or good to bad, skilled to unskilled, and so forth). If this is possible, we refer to the resulting scale as an "ordinal scale."

The defining characteristic of an ordinal scale lies in what is called its transitive property: if A is greater than B (written A > B), and B greater than C, then A must be greater than C. If this does not hold for all individuals, then we do not have a legitimate ordinal scale. We know of situations in sports where A can beat B, B can beat C, but yet C can beat A. In such instances we might intuitively suspect that there is more than one dimension involved, and we cannot obtain a unique ordering or ranking.

In many instances social scientists must settle for rather crude ordinal scales in which there are numerous ties. A sociologist may have divided families roughly into one of six social classes, which he may have termed the "lower-lower," the "upper-lower," the "lower-middle," the "upper-middle," the "lower-upper," and the "upper-upper" classes. Clearly, a prestige ordering is implied in this terminology, but there will be large numbers of individuals who are treated as being tied and are placed in the same class. Whenever such ties occur, there is always the question of whether they are really ties or whether these ties merely reflect the crudity of the measuring instrument. Usually it is the latter. Few sociologists hold to the position that one can find a fixed number of distinct social classes composed of completely homogeneous (or tied) individuals. They recognize that there is a continuous gradation of statuses and that they have arbitrarily decided to use six rather than some other number of classes.

INTERVAL AND RATIO SCALES

At times it is possible to utilize a standard unit of measure, such as the pound, foot, second, or dollar, thus making it possible to speak about the numerical sizes of the differences among scores. These kinds of measures are most common in the physical sciences, but there are some available to the social scientist as well. An obvious one is the monetary unit. Time may also be used as the basis of such a unit, as for example the number of years of formal schooling or the amount of time spent watching TV. Whenever social scientists compare different kinds of communities, the relative numbers of certain types of people can be used as the basis of the unit. Cities may be contrasted with respect to relative numbers of non-whites, the percentage of the labor force in manufacturing, the proportion of homes with running water, and so on.

When such objective units exist, it becomes possible to compare differences. For example, if A's income is $20,000, if B's is $14,000, and C's is $8,000, we can say that B's income is halfway between A's and C's, or equivalently that if there were another person with the same income as B's, then his income plus B's would exactly equal the sum of A's and C's. Such an operation would be inappropriate in the case of prestige. One cannot add the prestige of A to that of C in any meaningful sense. Whenever it is possible to compare differences in scores because of the existence of such a standardized unit, we refer to the scale as an "interval scale."

If, in addition, there is a nonarbitrary zero point, it then becomes possible to compare the ratio of two scores, and we have what is termed a "ratio scale." In practice, whenever we have a definite unit of measurement, such as the dollar or inch, we will in fact have a meaningful zero point (no income or no length). In these cases we may also compare ratios and make meaningful statements, such as that one person's income is twice that of another.[1]

Of course, the aim of all scientists is to improve measure-

---

[1] Perhaps the most familiar example of an interval scale which is not at the same time a ratio scale is temperature as measured in terms of either centigrade or Fahrenheit scales. Since the zero points on both of these scales are arbitrary, one does not speak in terms of 40° as being twice as hot as 20°, though it *is* meaningful to compare this difference with the difference between, say, 80° and 60°.

ment as much as possible and to utilize as many interval or ratio scales as is feasible, given limitations of knowledge and cost. But it is often extremely difficult in the social sciences to obtain true interval or ratio scales, though ordinal scales are much more frequent. One of the most challenging tasks confronting the social scientist is that of improving his measurement, and a number of rather ingenious though indirect procedures have been developed toward that end.

The major point I wish to emphasize in the present context is that it is by no means a simple task even to conceptualize what our variables or scales should be. The usual process seems to involve beginning with relatively obvious manifest characteristics that yield nothing better than nominal scales and cross-classifications. Then when one finds certain of these to be useful, in the sense of enabling him to predict to other variables or classifications, he must begin the more difficult task of conceptualizing the variables that underlie or explain these simple relationships. At the same time, he must find practical ways of measuring them as well as he can.

The first step is therefore that of using manifest relationships, plus whatever intuitive insights one may have, to develop theories involving more abstract variables with greater explanatory power. Such theories will be discussed in the following chapter. We turn next to a consideration of the kinds of exploratory research that are usually necessary to lay the groundwork for this kind of theorizing. The major objective of such exploratory research is that of selecting out a relatively small number of possible variables, or categories, from the extremely large number that can be developed. To do this, the investigator must become immersed in the data, and he must rely very heavily on his own insights and intuition, without benefit of any well defined scientific principles as guidelines. As I shall emphasize throughout, exploratory studies are literally just that. They are beginnings, not ends in themselves. After the beginning has been made, there are many opportunities for more rigorous methodological principles to serve as useful guidelines.

Participant Observation

Suppose a social scientist wishes to study something about which he knows practically nothing or about which there seem to be numerous misconceptions. Or perhaps the phenomenon is so familiar, so close to home, that there are aspects of it that everyone is likely to miss. How can he proceed? Clearly the research must be highly exploratory. It cannot rely on specific hypotheses or a relatively small list of variables that are likely to be significant. The investigator must immerse himself in the data, learn all he can from as many perspectives as possible, and obtain very general information rather than data limited to a rather narrow focus.

The general label which exploratory research of this nature has been given is that of "participant observation." This term actually refers to a rather wide range of activities varying from actually becoming a bona fide member of the group being studied to observing and interviewing its members rather informally as an outsider. The basic prerequisite of all participant observation, however, is that the social scientist must gain the confidence of the persons being studied, so that his presence does not disrupt or in any way interfere with the natural course of events and so that they will provide him with honest answers to his questions and not hide important activities from his view.

Anthropologists are probably the most frequent users of this approach, so much so that participant observation is sometimes erroneously identified with the anthropological approach. Obviously, if an anthropologist is studying a primitive tribe for the first time, he will have very little idea what to expect in terms of the specifics of the situation, though he may know what has been learned about other similar tribes. He may, in fact, have a good many working hypotheses concerning ways in which variables are interrelated and what he can expect to find in his "society." He would be very surprised, for example, to find a highly elaborated political system or a hierarchical religious organization in a tribe whose economy consisted of hunting and gathering and a rather communistic system of distribution. If, in fact, he were to find this juxtaposition of hierarchical religious organization and simple economy, he might very well suspect that missionaries had been at work.

It is thus almost impossible for a reasonably well-read social scientist to enter the situation with a completely open mind and with no hunches whatsoever as to what he will find. The general strategy of participant observation, however, is that the social scientist should attempt to purge himself of as many preconceptions as possible, that he should deliberately collect as wide a range of facts as is feasible, and that he should not begin sifting these facts and interpreting them until he has become very familiar with the general life pattern of the people being studied.

One problem with participant observation, as can readily be imagined, is that it is very difficult to lay down specific guidelines as to how this can be accomplished. Participant observation depends very much on the interpersonal skills of the investigator and on his ability to prevent his own preconceptions from distorting his interpretations. Given the fact that the situation is wide open to such distortions, either intentional or unintentional, there is an obvious need for replication of each piece of research by several investigators. Before returning to this point, however, let us consider several additional examples of field research involving participant observation.

One of the earlier sociological studies that represents the extreme form of active participation, in which one totally immerses himself in the data, was carried out by Nels Anderson.[2] Anderson wanted to study the life of the hobo and could think of no better way to accomplish this than to become one himself. He traveled about from city to city, living in various hobohemias, flophouses, and mission homes. In doing so he gradually accumulated numerous insights into such things as the status distinctions among hoboes, how they

[2] See Nels Anderson, *The Hobo* (Chicago: University of Chicago Press, 1923).

communicated, their life style, and something about the stages that a man was likely to go through as he passed from being an occasional worker to a "bum." The resulting study is still fascinating to read and contains numerous insights that could not possibly have been obtained by a respectable middle-class survey interviewer.

Participant observation is ideally suited for studying various forms of deviant or lower-class behavior, where problems of establishing good rapport are especially difficult. Few social scientists are in a position to become an actual member of the group itself, as Anderson did. They would give themselves away, they might have the wrong skin color, or they may not wish to engage in the form of deviant behavior being studied. One would hardly expect a female social scientist to become a prostitute in order to study prostitution. It is often possible, however, to work into the natural setting in such a way that after an initial period of suspicion and curiosity, the social scientist becomes trusted and even useful as a confidant and adviser.

An early classic study of this type was conducted by William F. Whyte, who studied lower-class street-corner life in Boston.[3] Whyte made no secret of the fact that he was a social scientist, but he tried to act as naturally as possible in the lower-class setting. He hung out at places frequented by young males, developed important contacts with local small-time politicians, gamblers, and gang leaders, and participated in the regular activities of one of the informal gangs.

More recently, a similar kind of study has been conducted by a white anthropologist, Elliot Liebow, on the lower-class black male.[4] Obviously, Liebow could not "pass" as a local community member, and it might be thought that the presence of a white would be disruptive of the normal interaction patterns at a local take-out restaurant which Liebow called "Tally's Corner." The essential strategy was to work himself

[3] See William F. Whyte, *Street Corner Society* (Chicago: University of Chicago Press, 1943).
[4] See Elliot Liebow, *Tally's Corner* (Boston: Little, Brown and Co., 1967).

into the local scene so that his presence became taken for granted and so that he could ask questions without seeming to be too inquisitive. By piecing together bits of information from conversations about wives, children, lovers, their work (or lack of work), and general daily routine, Liebow was able to produce a very vivid account of what it is like to be a lower-class black male, with no place to go and with no realistic expectations of a future any different from the present.

In Liebow's study, as in all others involving participant observation, there is the obvious impossibility of studying "everything." Eventually, the social scientist must order his data to make sense out of them. Unfortunately, there are few if any general guidelines for doing this except by analogy with previous studies or common practice. Liebow, for example, decided to organize his book around relationships of his heroes with various others: relationships focused around work, with wives or common-law partners, with their children, with other women, and with each other. Obviously, a second social scientist might have chosen to present his findings in another way.

One of the fundamental difficulties with participant observation, as should be obvious from these few illustrative examples, is the lack of standardization usually involved. Each social scientist is like a journalist writing his own story; there is little guarantee that several such journalists will report the same story. As mentioned previously, replication is the obvious answer to this difficulty, but replication is not always easy to accomplish. Let us consider some of the reasons why this is the case.

One of the fundamental reasons that replications have been relatively rare in the social sciences is, frankly, that social scientists have not been sufficiently convinced of their need to provide the necessary rewards for such studies. Many social scientists have been trained in humanistic fields where literary style and novelty are premium qualities, and the thought that someone is "merely" doing the study over again is likely to lead to serious questions concerning his scientific integrity. Why isn't he moving on to something new? He needs to show his originality! Present practices in graduate training programs are also at fault; graduate students are told that they must be original, and book publishers and journal editors reinforce this practice by not encouraging replication studies. Given the fact that there is so much to study and so few social scientists, the result has been a spreading out to new subjects rather than a thorough, systematic, and tedious examination of the old.

Another more fundamental difficulty with replication studies is the fact that if a second investigator were to study the same group or society, there would be differences from the first investigator's findings simply because the group had changed. Therefore it would be difficult to distinguish real changes from measurement differences. If scientific laws existed for predicting such changes, then corrections could be made so that measurement artifacts could be discovered. We have a version of the chicken and egg problem here. With good theories we could separate real change from measurement error. But we need good measurement in order to verify the theories. This problem will be discussed in greater detail in Chapter 5, since it is not peculiar to the participant-observation approach.

A second form of replication, which is far more practical, given the fact that human beings object to being observed over and over again, involves conducting numerous studies on similar groups to see if similar conclusions are reached. If they are, then we have more faith in the findings. But if they are not, we are again faced with the problem of deciding whether the differences are due to measurement error or to real differences. In this second form of replication, we are not concerned with changes in the same group, but with variability among groups. Again, if we were able to assume that all groups are alike, or that they differ in known ways, we could assess the degree to which differences actually found were due to differences in measurement, techniques of observation, or other factors introduced by the investigator himself. If we knew there were no differences in measurements, we could assess the degree to which the groups actually differed. But if we lack both kinds of information, we are kept guessing as to the sources of the differences found.

In general, techniques of participant observation are extremely useful in providing initial insights and hunches that can lead to more careful formulations of the problem and explicit hypotheses. But they are open to the charge that findings may be idiosyncratic and difficult to replicate. Therefore many social scientists prefer to think of participant observation as being very useful at a certain stage in the research process rather than being an approach that yields a finished piece of research. Unfortunately, many excellent exploratory studies have not been followed up more systematically. A book such as *Tally's Corner* seems to stand by itself, so to speak, and is not taken as a starting point for further research.

This situation is partly the fault of social scientists themselves for not attempting to spell out the implications more explicitly in order to investigate hypotheses more systematically. But it is also due to the fact that the guidelines for moving from such exploratory research to more systematic and standardized approaches are not very well spelled out, and there are not enough social scientists to follow up all the leads that are uncovered by such exploratory research. As we shall see, the systematic investigation of even a rather simple hypothesis can be very expensive and time-consuming, and not enough resources have been made available for this kind of careful work.

The Sample Survey

A possible compromise between the exploratory research of the single participant observer and a much more systematic standardized approach is the descriptive sample survey. One of the nagging problems raised by any small-scale research is that of the generalizability of one's findings. How typical of primitive tribes are the Oscotch? How typical is "Tally's Corner" of the hangouts of black males throughout the urban United States? And how comparable are the data collection techniques of two different investigators? Have they asked the same questions? Are there subtle differences in their working hypotheses or intellectual biases that affect the responses they get, not to mention the way they interpret their data?

In the sample survey or mailed questionnaire a premium is placed on certain kinds of standardization, so that the study may be replicated. The social scientist using this kind of research has three major methodological concerns. The first is to collect data in such a way that all respondents are confronted with nearly identical situations: similar interviewer relationships and the same set of questions. The second is a concern with sampling and the question of the generalizability of results. The third is with specifying standard criteria for data analysis procedures, so that different analysts will reach similar conclusions when confronted with the same set of data. Let us consider each of these forms of standardization in turn.

STANDARDIZATION OF DATA

If a large nation-wide survey were conducted, using perhaps one hundred interviewers, and if each interviewer were permitted to chat informally with whatever respondents he pleased, one can imagine the nature of the results. Interviewers could be expected to come up with "findings" that supported their own viewpoints. In effect, each would be his own social scientist, except for the fact that he would lack the proper training. Obviously, in a large-scale survey a certain degree of standardization is absolutely necessary. In fact, a careful survey involves a much higher degree of such standardization than most laymen would imagine. A considerable amount of time goes into careful training of interviewers, for example. There will be a large number of practice interviews, with periodic sessions at which the interviewers' problems and questions can be answered. A very lengthy interviewer's manual, containing detailed instructions for each question, will be studied very carefully, and many parts committed to memory. Interviewers are carefully instructed on how to "probe" when vague answers have been given and how to repeat questions so that they appear to be differently worded even though the wording is given exactly as before. They are told how to introduce themselves, how to locate the proper respondent in each household, and numerous other things. As the interviewers' completed schedules of answered questions are turned in, they are carefully checked for completeness, possible biases, or other inadequacies.

The wording of questions is a very crucial factor in survey research, and it will usually be necessary to develop several "pretests" before the final instrument is prepared. The interview schedule must be carefully planned so that it is interesting, not too long, and so that response errors and biases are kept to a minimum. As is true for experiments, it is often necessary to disguise the true purpose of the interview. Sometimes this is done by asking a number of questions that are of no inherent interest to the investigator, with the important questions interspersed so that their interconnection is not too obvious. Questions must be carefully worded so that a given answer does not imply two different things and so that respondents with varying amounts of formal education can all answer them equally well.

As can readily be imagined, standardization has a number of important disadvantages. One of the major ones is that the wording of the questions may "force" a respondent to give an answer that he does not fully endorse. Simple "yes" and "no" answers are obvious examples of forced choice responses, but there are much more complex ones. A respondent may be given a statement together with a list of five possible responses, then asked to give that response which comes closest to his own opinion. But suppose none of them do. Isn't the investigator putting words into his mouth? Why not let him talk freely about it and then attempt to classify his answers?

This is often accomplished by inserting what are called "open-ended" questions into the interview schedule. "Would you mind telling me *why* you feel that way, Mr. Jones?" The difficulty is that interviewers differ considerably in their ability and willingness to elicit really detailed answers to such questions. Mr. Jones may not know why he feels that way. Should the interviewer assume this and move on, or should he attempt to get him to answer by probing further? He might ask Mr. Jones to give a few examples and then ask him "why" in the context of these examples. It is likely to be found that in many interview schedules the "open-ended" questions will not be answered, whereas a few will contain lengthy essays. If the latter can be used to provide additional insights or interesting quotations, then they may be useful for that purpose, but the problem of typicality or generalizability again arises.

Perhaps a more satisfactory procedure, and one that is commonly used, is to utilize the pretests for these more exploratory formulations, gradually working toward closed or forced-choice answers that are not too restrictive. For example, if the aim is to provide the respondent with five or six alternative answers that are most likely to give a fairly inclusive range of possibilities, the first group of respondents (on a pretest) might be given a completely open question, to which they were asked to write essay answers. On the basis of these answers, the investigator could then attempt to construct a set of alternative responses that represented perhaps 90 per cent of the answers he had found on the pretest. A second pretest could then be given which included his list of five alternative answers plus a space for additional ones. A skillful interviewer could then probe to ascertain whether the list was sufficiently inclusive or whether it contained any ambiguities not previously noted. The final version of the question might contain three of the previous alternative answers, plus modifications of the other two, plus a sixth alternative that had not been anticipated as a result of the first pretest.

The push toward standardization of questions can produce a false sense of security in many situations. Although questions may be worded in the same way for all respondents, this does not guarantee that they will interpret them the same way. Some may see them as threatening or too personal and may deliberately falsify their answers or refuse to cooperate. Others may not take the task seriously enough and may give almost random responses or ones that they find amusing or that might upset the investigator. Still others may not understand the wording or may interpret the questions differently from the way the investigator intended. A good deal can be learned from the pretest situation, particularly if respondents are given a chance to react to the interview situation. Did they find the questions interesting? Which ones did they find difficult to answer? Why? Were some too personal? What did they think were the objectives of the study? And how did they think it could be improved?

It is perhaps a rather surprising finding that, in general, most respondents seem to enjoy the interview experience and appear to take it seriously. Furthermore, it has been found that they seem to give honest answers to questions that many of us would take to be highly personal—questions about sex practices, religious beliefs, prejudices, and political attitudes. Out-and-out refusals to be interviewed are relatively rare, being no more than 1 or 2 per cent in many studies. One of the major obstacles faced in many surveys is the initial resistance to being interviewed, either because the respondent does not wish to be bothered or because he fears some trick. (A serious threat to survey research is the salesman who is instructed to introduce himself as a person taking surveys of reading habits, only later to divulge the fact that he is actually selling encyclopedias or magazines.) Once the interview is actually underway, it is generally found that the vast majority of respondents are extremely cooperative.

There are, of course, only certain kinds of facts that can be studied by means of survey interviews or mailed questionnaires. These instruments are best designed to obtain present attitudes about relatively simple phenomena. They cannot be used to study actual behavior as it takes place. Frequently a respondent is asked to recall how he behaved (or felt) at some previous time, but it is recognized that numerous distortions can creep into such recollections. Most of us could not accurately describe our behavior even on the previous day, to say nothing of estimating how much time we spend "on the average" doing gardening or reading books. We can recall how we voted in the previous election, but often it seems advisable to say that we voted with the majority when in fact we did not. Because everyone is expected to vote, we may claim that we voted when we actually only intended to do so. Since it would obviously be impossible to observe each adult in the process of voting, to say nothing of his sexual behavior, the social scientist has little choice but to rely on verbal statements.

Most surveys involve a single interview with each respondent, making it impossible to study directly any changes in his attitudes. Of course it is possible to ask a respondent how he felt last September, or three years ago, but the recall of attitudes is especially difficult and subject to distortions of various kinds. Therefore it is often desirable to use what are termed "panel" surveys, in which a given set of respondents is interviewed at two or more different points in time. It has been found that respondents tire of this process rather quickly, as might be expected, and that therefore the attrition rates in panel studies are very high. However, it is possible by careful sampling techniques to work out rotation systems so that, at each successive interviewing period, only a fixed proportion of respondents have been interviewed once or twice before. This compromise procedure enables the social scientist to study attitude changes while not placing too much of a burden on any given set of respondents.

PROBABILITY SAMPLING

We have seen that one of the major problems with exploratory research, which must be based on relatively small and carefully selected samples, is that it is difficult to decide just how typical the cases are. This could be resolved to some degree by replication, but we have also seen that participant observation studies are difficult to replicate. In the case of sample surveys considerable attention is ordinarily given to sampling procedures. These procedures will usually involve what is referred to as a probability sample. The essential feature of a probability sample is that each individual in the entire population, to which a generalization is being made, must have a *known* probability of appearing in the sample. Before considering several kinds of probability sampling procedures, let us discuss in a general way why sampling is so important.

Suppose you have been told on a news report that a survey has been conducted showing that 60 per cent of the Protestants sampled intended to vote Republican, whereas only 40 per cent of the Catholics expected to vote Republican. Of course you might want to know the implications of this fact for the final vote tabulation, in which case it would be necessary to know the proportions of Protestants and Catholics in the area. But let us assume that you are primarily interested in this difference, which amounts to 20 per cent and which seems to require some kind of explanation.

What are the questions you should ask? First, you would wish to know how the sample was selected. Were these simply friends of the announcer, or were they selected "scientifically"? Another question is: "How accurate are the responses in terms of the way people will actually vote"? We shall here assume that this particular question can be answered by pointing to previous successes in predicting voting behavior from such surveys. The specific question I should like to deal with involves the size of the sample. Consider the situations in the accompanying tables.

	Protestant	Catholic	Total		Protestant	Catholic	Total
Republican	3	2	5		6	4	10
Democrat	2	3	5		4	6	10
Total	5	5	10		10	10	20

	Protestant	Catholic	Total		Protestant	Catholic	Total
Republican	30	20	50		60	40	100
Democrat	20	30	50		40	60	100
Total	50	50	100		100	100	200

	Protestant	Catholic	Total
Republican	600	400	1000
Democrat	400	600	1000
Total	1000	1000	2000

The figures in the body of each table refer to the actual numbers of people sampled. In the first table there are only ten people in all, whereas there are two thousand in the last table. In every table, however, the percentages of Protestants and Catholics favoring the Republicans are 60 and 40 respectively.

Clearly, one would not have much faith in the generalizability of the results of the first two tables, containing ten and twenty cases respectively. But what about the third? The fourth? Just what are the chances of finding a 20 per cent difference between Protestants and Catholics in each instance? Intuition would be a very poor guide here, although it seems "obvious" that one should have more faith that a real difference exists within the larger population in the case of the last table than in the first. But exactly what is meant by this statement, and how does one go about pinning down the odds?

This is a problem in statistical inference, a relatively complex field based on the mathematical laws of probability. In this simple kind of example the probabilities can be specified *if* the method of sampling has been a proper one. But if we do not know how the cases were selected, nothing much can be said. If we know that the sample is a "random" sample (see below), then we may say that if there were in fact no difference in the larger population between the percentages of Protestants and Catholics preferring the Republicans, then the chances are very high that sampling fluctuations alone could account for the results of the first two tables. The chances of getting a 20 per cent sample difference in the third table are about one in twenty (written $P = .05$); for the fourth they are less than one in a hundred ($P < .01$), and for the fifth table they are infinitesimal.[5]

It would be nice if we could attain certainty, but unless we collected data on the entire population this result would be impossible. Given the huge size of the voting population, such an aim would obviously be impractical. But we see from these particular examples that there are some general principles that make it possible to give precise probabilities of particular sets of outcomes which, together with any information we might have about measurement accuracy, give us a rational basis for evaluating the confidence we have in the survey results.

One general principle is intuitively obvious. Other things being equal, the larger the sample the more confidence we have that sample results (e.g., a 20 per cent difference) will approximate the true figures for the population. Less obvious is the point that it is the *size* of the sample that counts, not the proportion of the population that it represents. This state-

---

[5] Procedures for computing such probabilities in simple tables of this sort are discussed under the heading of "chi-square" in practically all textbooks on applied statistics. The crucial point is that all such computations require the assumption that a probability sampling procedure has been used and that measurement error is negligible.

ment is not quite true if the sample becomes almost as large as the population, but it is a very good approximation. If the sample is really a random one, we have just as much faith in the results of the fifth table, regardless of whether the population contains twenty thousand or twenty million persons. This runs counter to the common sense argument people sometimes raise to the effect that surveys can't really be any good because they themselves have never been asked for their opinions. It is in fact possible to get very good estimates of voting intentions from a sample of two thousand, even where one is dealing with the entire population of the United States. Naturally, only a small *proportion* of people would be selected in such a sample.

Another principle that is consistent with common sense is that the bigger the difference found in the sample, the less likely it is that this difference could have occurred purely by chance, other things being equal. In our example we are assuming a 20 per cent difference, but perhaps it might have been 10 per cent or 30 per cent. However, common sense is not very good at telling us whether we should have more faith in a 20 per cent difference with four hundred cases or a 30 per cent difference with two hundred cases. These kinds of questions can only be answered by the statistician.

Finally, the amount of faith we should have in a given size difference for a fixed sample size is also a function of the *kind* of probability sample that has been drawn. Let us therefore consider briefly three kinds of probability samples that are often combined in complex surveys but are at least analytically distinct. In complex sample surveys, where combinations are used, the formulas for calculating probabilities can become fairly complex, but fortunately we do not need to concern ourselves with these matters.

The simplest kind of probability sample conceptually is the "random" sample. In a random sample all combinations of persons have an equal probability of being selected. This also means that each individual has the same chance of being selected as any other individual. Random samples can be selected by obtaining a complete listing of all population members and then using a table of random numbers or some other random device for selecting them. In practice, this is equivalent to drawing names from a hat, balls from an urn, or cards from a well shuffled deck. But it is a bit more exact, since pieces of paper may stick together, and shuffling is always imperfect.

It is important to recognize that random sampling does not refer to hit-or-miss sampling. One cannot obtain a random sample by interviewing the first hundred people he sees on the street corner or by accepting the first one hundred telephone responses to a radio appeal. Think about the possible biases this kind of sampling can produce. Obviously, the person who never visits the street corner or turns on his radio has no chance of being selected. Remember that we must know the chances of each person's being selected in order to calculate probabilities. We cannot know this without some kind of listing and a random device for pulling names from this list.

A second kind of probability sample is the "stratified" sample, which also involves a random selection procedure *within* each of several strata or groupings of individuals. The most common reason why we first group individuals and then select a certain number of cases within each grouping is that we may wish to compare the groups, and a purely random sample might not provide enough cases for doing this. If one wanted to compare Jews with Protestants, a straight random sample of two hundred persons might yield only ten Jews selected by chance. As an alternative, one might obtain separate lists of Protestants and Jews (the two strata) and sample one hundred randomly from each list. Obviously, the principles of stratification can be extended to multiple groupings. One might subdivide his population into four strata: white-collar Protestants, white-collar Jews, blue-collar Protestants, and blue-collar Jews, selecting fifty cases from each. There are also some other more subtle advantages of using stratified samples, but this is not the place to discuss them.

It should be recognized that stratified samples will ordinarily not give every individual an equal chance of being selected. In our example, the Jews will be deliberately oversampled, since we wish to obtain enough of them to compare them with the Protestants. That is, each Jew will have a higher probability of being selected than each Protestant. Perhaps the sample will consist of one hundred Protestants from a list of ten thousand and one hundred Jews from a list of two hundred. Then each Protestant has one chance in a hundred of being sampled, and each Jew has one chance in two. Since this fact is known, however, and since each Protestant who happens to be sampled represents ninety-nine others, whereas each Jew in the sample represents only one other Jew, the statistician can correct for this known bias by introducing the proper weights in his analysis.

The third type of probability sample is actually the most practical one in large-scale surveys. Lists of American voters simply do not exist. Even city directories get out of date very rapidly, and most counties do not have accurate lists of their residents. (Many lists, such as telephone directories and auto registration lists, are obviously biased in favor of middle-class and upper-class individuals.) There are, however, lists of counties within the United States or census tracts and blocks within cities. A random sample of such counties or blocks might first be selected. If the resulting geographic area is still very large, the selected areas (e.g., counties) can be subdivided and sub-areas again randomly selected. Finally, a random (or stratified) sample may be selected from within those areas that have been previously selected.

This form of sampling is referred to as "cluster" or "area" sampling and is much more complex than the previous two kinds. Its obvious advantage is that it saves the cost of obtaining complete lists. Only those counties or census tracts that have been selected (randomly) need to be subdivided still further. Also, there will be considerable savings on interviewer costs. In a nation-wide sample it would obviously be extremely costly to send trained interviewers all over the country to pick up a few interviews here and there (perhaps five in Montana, three in Nevada, and one in Alaska). But having selected, say, fifty counties at random, and then selected individuals within each of these counties, the investigator can make each interviewer responsible for only one or two counties.

The problem with such cluster samples is that one must avoid extremely homogeneous clusters or areas. A film made several years ago about a so-called typical town in the Midwest that was found to represent the rest of the country involved a number of humorous episodes when this fact was learned. Needless to say, the town's typicality was soon destroyed. This is an example of the extreme form of a cluster sample (one cluster) that might be ideal from the standpoint of saving interviewing costs. But it depends on the community being heterogeneous enough so that all viewpoints are represented in exactly their proper proportions. Of course we know that no such single communities exist, but perhaps a set of ten or twenty could be found. The opposite extreme would be the community that is perfectly homogeneous, so that any one individual is exactly like the rest. Then we would only need to interview one person to know everything, and even though we interviewed two thousand our effective sample size would be only one! Needless to say, the selection of this kind of community in our sample could give rise to extremely misleading results—either two thousand Republicans or two thousand Democrats.

It does turn out that people who live close together tend to be relatively similar with respect to many of the variables social scientists wish to study: education, income levels, political preferences, or prejudice levels. Yet they are rarely completely homogeneous. Therefore it becomes necessary to juggle the economic advantages of their proximity with the degree to which they are so homogeneous that it would be unwise to interview more than a small number of persons from each area. As can be imagined, the problems of selecting an optimum sample become highly complex at this stage and require the experience of experts.

One important general point should be made before leaving the subject of sampling. Once the sample has been selected by sound principles, it becomes essential that a very high percentage of those who have been selected by probability means actually be interviewed and their responses used in the survey. If they may select themselves out of the survey for varying reasons, then the probability nature of the sampling procedure is destroyed. Suppose, for example, that 20 per cent refused to be interviewed and another 20 per cent could not be located because they were not at home at convenient times of the day. Since we would not know very much about these individuals, other than that they refused or were not at home, we could not claim that we knew the probabilities of each type being actually selected (and used) in the survey. All kinds of unknown biases might creep into the study. Some refusals will always occur, and it is the task of methodological studies to determine in a general way the kinds of biases these are likely to introduce. But there is no substitute for a response rate of at least 80 to 90 per cent. This means that interviewers must employ interpersonal skills and be persistent in calling back, perhaps as many as five or six times, in order to locate people who are rarely at home.

STANDARDIZATION OF ANALYSIS

It is not only desirable to standardize the collection of data and sampling procedures, but it is also highly important to specify general rules for analyzing data. Otherwise, the biases of the investigator may again play a major role in the final product. Many readers are basically unsympathetic to tables and statistical summaries. They want interesting descriptions of real cases and quotations of just what "typical" people had to say. While there is no denying that such case studies and quotes do help to portray the results in a vivid way and to provide additional insights, they may give a very misleading impression unless supplemented by numerical results.

In a sense, numerical tabulations are more "democratic"; they involve the "one-man-one-vote" principle. Quotations may be used selectively to give the wrong impression. A few very vocal respondents may be quoted to the exclusion of the rest. When we read the remarks of a "typical" respondent, we must rely on the writer's judgment as to which respondents are really typical. In effect, only part of the total information is being used, and the advantages of careful sampling and attention to selection biases are nullified.

As long as we are dealing with purely descriptive surveys,

as is the case in the present discussion, there are well defined procedures of analysis that can be used to guard against selection biases in the analysis stage. These range from very simple tabular analyses to complex statistical procedures for combining large numbers of variables into a single equation. Basically, these procedures provide ways of boiling down or summarizing the data so that they can be described in terms of a small number of summary measures such as percentages, means, standard deviations (a measure of heterogeneity), and various kinds of correlation coefficients that measure the degree to which two variables are associated with each other. If the investigator wants to claim that high X's (say, prejudice levels) go along with high values of Y (say, political conservatism), he may give a correlation coefficient and an equation linking the two. Or he may provide the reader with a series of tables involving percentages, showing that some percentage differences are larger than others.

One common myth among laymen, students, and many social scientists is that the presentation of numerical facts somehow or another prevents or inhibits one from also gaining insights as to the "true nature" of the relationship, which can only be experienced by some kind of a "gut feeling" for the data. This is utter nonsense. What often happens, of course, is that the numerical results do not coincide with the insights obtained by an intuitive inspection of the data. So much the worse, then, for "intuition." But there is nothing whatsoever in tables alone that prevents one from using his intuition to arrive at meaningful explanations for the findings. In fact, a series of tables that give peculiar combinations of results may literally cry out for an explanation that requires considerable insight. It seems to me that many persons who use this kind of argument are either too lazy to read the tables or to follow the statistical arguments, or else they would like to be in the enviable position of not having to make their intuitive arguments be compatible with the data.

There is, however, a sense in which the proponents of nonquantitative social science seem to be justified. Many survey reports have in fact stopped with a presentation of tables and correlations, with only very brief and inadequate interpretations of what might lie behind the data, so to speak. That is, they are essentially descriptive rather than analytic. They tell a reader how he may *predict* to voting behavior (i.e., throw together the right combinations of variables) without ever trying to understand this behavior by giving a theoretical explanation of the data. This is not a defect of quantitative approaches per se, but of the rather limited objectives of the survey. The same criticism can often be applied to studies using participant observation. The reader is given a vivid description of the lower-class black or the drug addict without any fully explicit theoretical explanation. We shall consider this kind of question in the next chapter.

We can argue somewhat as follows, however. The investigator is usually focusing on one dependent variable that he wishes to "explain." Sometimes these are social problem variables such as delinquency rates, discrimination, population growth, and the like. But they may not have been selected with any practical objectives in mind. Certain variables will undoubtedly be found to be *correlated* with these dependent variables. If looked at in terms of percentages, this means that there will be large percentage differences using these variables. If interval scales have been used, there will be minimal scatter about smooth curves describing the relationship between X and Y, as in Figure 1 of Chapter 2. Even if these associations are strong, there is always the possibility that in small samples they may be due to chance fluctuations, or what is referred to as "sampling error." That is, a replication using a different sample might give very different results. If probability sampling has been used, the investigator may apply rather stringent tests to rule out the chance argument. He may also place what are called "confidence intervals" around his results, to give the reader a good idea of the accuracy of his estimates. For example, he may say that the probability is .95 that the Republican candidate will get 56 per cent of the vote, plus or minus 3 per cent.

If the chance explanation has been ruled out on probability grounds, and *if* the correlation between two variables is high enough, the investigator may then infer that he may have something worth talking about. He has located a possible explanatory factor and can then begin the more difficult task of making theoretical sense out of his correlations. On the other hand, if none of his variables turn out to be related (beyond chance limits) to the variable(s) he is trying to explain, then he knows that he must look elsewhere. Perhaps he has the wrong set of variables altogether. Perhaps his measurement has been so poor that only improved measurement could show up strong enough correlations. Or perhaps there are so many factors at work that he will need to include 30 or 40 simultaneously before he stands any chance of arriving at a satisfactory explanation. The advantage of quantitative procedures is that one can obtain a good idea of just what potential is in the data.

As already implied, the procedures for arriving at these rather minimal tests and descriptive measures are rather well worked out. The basic gaps that now exist seem to be in two principal areas. One is in the area of measurement, and in particular the problem of inferring indirectly what is going on behind the scenes (e.g., in people's minds) on the basis of measured indicators of the variables in which we are really interested. The second area where precise guidelines are difficult to lay down is one that involves the linking of descriptive facts (whether quantitative or not) with our causal interpretations or theories as to the mechanisms that have produced these facts.

In both areas there is an obvious need for clear-cut and explicit rules of the game that will prevent an analyst from giving almost any interpretation he pleases to a given set of facts. When one jokes about there being liars, damned liars, and statisticians, I presume he is referring to the apparent fact that a given set of data may be interpreted in many different ways. Actually this is a gross distortion of the role of the statistician, who is a very honest guardian of our scientific morality. But we shall see in the next chapter that in a certain sense there *are* many different ways of interpreting the same set of data, though the guidelines are much more specific than this kind of naive joke would seem to imply. But although they are specific, they are both highly technical and difficult to apply in practice.

4

Explanation
and
Theory

With time and effort, fact upon fact can be assembled. But do facts speak for themselves? Some people have argued that they do, but unfortunately facts often speak in so many languages that the resulting babel of voices becomes understandable only after they can be simplified and reduced to manageable proportions. How can such reduction be carried out? What facts are "unimportant" or "irrelevant"? Can each party to a dispute seize upon whatever set of facts it chooses, so that there is no scientific way of resolving the dispute? It would be convenient if the answer were a simple "no," but, as we shall see, there is a certain sense in which facts can never stand alone.

A theoretical explanation will inevitably contain assumptions, some of which are inherently untestable whereas others cannot be tested in terms of the particular data at hand. These assumptions *plus* the facts become the guides the scientist must follow, and the assumptions are always fallible and subject to modification. The development of a science consists of substituting increasingly realistic and more useful assumptions, so that the resulting theoretical explanation accounts for an increasing variety of facts and yields more and more precise predictions that can be tested in terms of the data.

In the context of the kinds of data discussed in the previous chapter, a social scientist may find that a number of variables are correlated or associated with the variable he wishes to explain. But he cannot leap from this factual result to the conclusion that they are the causes of the phenomenon in question. In effect, there will be many more correlates of a phenomenon than there are causes, and the task then becomes that of reducing the number of explanatory variables by eliminating those that are related to the dependent variable by happenstance or because of the common influence of another variable.

At best, this process of making causal inferences is a difficult and technical task. The most tempting thing to do is to select certain of the correlates by fiat as the "true causes" and then to muster as many emotional reasons as possible in defense of one's position. The trouble is that persons with different biases or vested interests are equally capable of producing convincing arguments—convincing, that is, to persons of their own persuasion. Social scientists have been particularly guilty of this kind of behavior, though many are seriously groping for more objective procedures less open to the influence of personal biases.

The obvious example of the dispute over cigarette smoking and lung cancer should convince the reader that this kind of polemics is not only characteristic of social scientists but indicates that the problem is widespread and of basic importance. As we shall see, it springs from a fundamental limitation of the scientific method plus a number of rather serious obstacles that are especially characteristic of much nonexperimental research. But the difficulty is not insurmountable, though it seems to be a fact of scientific life that every time we do away with an objectionable assumption we must pay a certain price, either in terms of substituting another assumption that is somewhat more plausible or by expanding the research.

In the case of experimental research we saw that randomization plus the use of symmetrical designs take care of a good many (though not all) such difficulties. In natural settings, as we have implied, variables come already interrelated and it is difficult to disentangle causes from effects. Sometimes we may observe phenomena to change according to a definite temporal sequence, in which case we may infer that the change which took place later certainly did not cause the prior change. But in many cases changes in all variables take place more or less continuously or so rapidly that we cannot observe them. In other instances the investigator may lack the funds or the time to study these changes. In all these situations his task is much more difficult than that of the experimenter, and he may have to substitute one or more untestable assumptions for an observed fact.

An Example

Before considering a number of abstract illustrations of complications that may arise in nonexperimental research, let us return to the example of the vicious cycle of poverty introduced in Chapter 1. In any relatively complex real-life situation there will be numerous variables operating, thus necessitating our dealing with different kinds or classes of factors more or less simultaneously. Suppose we have been able to identify six very general kinds of variables that we think are related approximately as indicated in Figure 3. In this particular model we are assuming that factors associated with a person's family affecting his basic personality are in Block I. These factors are assumed to influence his specific prejudices (Block II), which in turn affect his actual behavior toward the minority (Block IV). This line of reasoning is a more or less orthodox social-psychological explanation of discrimination. But there

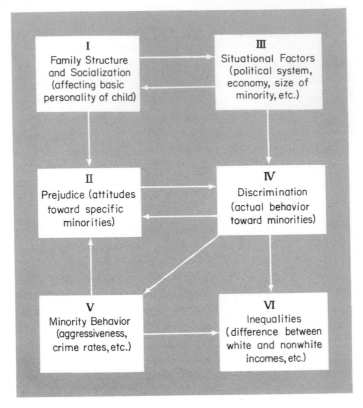

Figure 3

may also be numerous situational factors (Block III) which also influence discrimination and which are causally linked to family background factors in Block I. Sociologists are more prone to emphasize Block III variables than prejudice and family socialization.

But the actual behavior of the minority also may affect both prejudice (Block II) and any inequalities that may exist between the minority and the dominant group (Block VI). The explanation of the "sophisticated conservative" involves assumed causal connections that emphasize the influence of Block V on Blocks II and VI, whereas that of the "sophisticated liberal" stresses the effects of Block IV (discrimination) on Blocks V and VI. It is of course possible to form a synthesis by arguing that "all" factors are important, but does this mean they are *equally* important? How can we assess the relative importance of each block of variables?

There are systematic ways of proceeding so as to attach numerical weights to each set of factors, but these all require careful conceptualization of the variables in each block, plus the accurate measurement of each variable. For example, if the variables in Block I are measured much more carefully than those in Block III, one should not be surprised to "discover" that family background factors turn out to be "more important" than the situational factors of Block III. Thus any study that is designed to evaluate the relative contributions of different sets of factors must be inclusive and thorough. Small-scale exploratory studies cannot be "added up" so as to achieve this effect.

What is the relevance of all this in terms of practical implications? Clearly, if we knew which sets of factors were most important in affecting discrimination or the behavior of a minority, this knowledge would be extremely useful as a guide to intelligent policy. Of course, certain kinds of variables may be more easily manipulated than others. Some may have direct effects on the status of the minority, whereas others may have indirect effects which, however, may be equally pronounced. If good quantitative data were available and a theory well established, we would be in a position to begin to answer applied questions of the following sort. How much would the median incomes of blacks be changed by the reduction of overall unemployment rates by 1 per cent? How much could we expect to change the aspiration levels of black youth if we were to invest an additional billion dollars in improved housing? How much if we were to invest the same amount in improving the school system in a specified way? Obviously we are not at present able to answer such questions with the degree of precision we would like, but they are at least potentially answerable with good data and a good theory.

In the following section we will confine our attention to models involving only a small number of variables in order to illustrate the basic principles involved. There is an extensive literature on the subject, particularly in the economics literature, for those persons with the necessary mathematics back-ground.[1]

Inferring Causal Relationships from Correlations

Suppose that two variables X and Y have been found to be correlated or associated and that we wish to claim that X is a cause of Y. Suppose also that we are willing to rule out the possibility that Y causes X (e.g., lung cancer causes smoking). To be specific, let us modify the example of Chapter 3 relating religious preference to political preference to give the following results:

	Protestants	*Catholics*	*Total*
Republicans	62	38	100
Democrats	38	62	100
Total	100	100	200

The figures in the body of the table are actual numbers of cases that, for convenience, have been selected to total to one hundred.

If we wanted to claim that political preference is (partly) caused by religious preference, we would have to worry about the "other things being equal" assumption. Since people are not assigned randomly to religious groupings, kept under rigid laboratory conditions, and later asked about political preferences, this kind of assumption is much less plausible than it would be in the case of experimental designs. Suppose, for example, that a person's occupation determined both his religious and his political preference. Then if occupation were held constant, the relationship between religion and politics might disappear. Perhaps the results might be as follows, if we constructed separate tables for white-collar and blue-collar occupations:

[1] Many of these references to the more technical literature are given in H. M. Blalock, Jr., *Causal Inferences in Nonexperimental Research* (Chapel Hill: University of North Carolina Press, 1964).

White-Collar:

	Protestants	Catholics	Total
Republicans	56	24	80
Democrats	14	6	20
Total	70	30	100

Blue-Collar:

	Protestants	Catholics	Total
Republicans	6	14	20
Democrats	24	56	80
Total	30	70	100

The first thing to notice about these two tables is that if white- and blue-collar respondents are combined, the resulting totals coincide exactly with those for the previous table. That is, the previous results have been decomposed so as to control for occupation. Every person in the first subtable is white collar, and therefore, within the limits of this crude dichotomy, occupation is being held constant. We see that there is no relationship between religion and political preference *within* either of the two subtables, since among white-collar respondents 80 per cent of both Protestants and Catholics are Republicans, whereas among the blue-collar group, 20 per cent of both denominations are Republicans. With a control for occupation, the original relationship has thus disappeared.

How can this have come about? One possible explanation is that the relationship between X and Y is spurious, which in Chapter 2 we diagramed as follows:

where Z represents the control variable, occupation. Common sense would suggest that if, in fact, Z were a common cause of both X and Y, then Z ought to be more strongly related to X and to Y than X and Y are to each other. We must remember that there will be numerous other causal factors operating. If we make the assumption that the aggregate effect of these variables produces random disturbances in both X and Y, then according to this model their correlation can only be accounted for by Z. If Z were held constant, there would be no reason to expect X and Y to remain associated.

This very simple argument can be stated much more rigorously, but it is essentially sound as far as it goes. We note, in fact, that in the above hypothetical data, occupation is strongly related to religion (70 per cent of the white-collar workers being Protestant, whereas only 30 per cent of the blue-collar workers are Protestant), and also to political preference (80 per cent of white-collar workers being Republican, as compared to 20 per cent of the blue-collar category). Thus we have found a plausible alternative explanation by locating a variable Z highly related to both X and Y, which is assumed to be a common cause. We would claim that the relationship between X and Y is spurious and due to Z.

How can an investigator get around this difficulty? In one sense it is impossible for him to do so, since a critic can always name a possible source of spuriousness. In fact, this is the game being played by the medical profession and the cigarette manufacturers, who claim that a proof of causation is lacking. It is important to realize that, strictly speaking, *no proof of causation is ever possible*, since there is no way that an investigator can guarantee that there is no variable producing a spurious relationship. This is another way of saying that there is no way of deciding that all possible causes have been controlled. As we have seen in Chapter 2, this also applies to experimental designs and is a fundamental limitation of *all* scientific research. This must be clearly recognized if unresolvable disputes are to be avoided.

Yet something must be done to convince the reasonable skeptic that the investigator has come up with a real cause of Y, not simply a correlate. In one sense, the burden of proof is on the investigator to explore as many plausible alternatives as is feasible, given the limitations imposed by his research design. The social scientist is well aware of this problem, and a careful study will always involve controls on numerous possible sources of spuriousness. Yet the critic may discover still another variable, at which point the burden of proof is on him to carry out a further study, control for this variable, and see if the original relationship can be reduced to zero. If this occurs the conclusions have to be revised. This factor emphasizes the tentative nature of all scientific work and justifies the cautious nature of scientific conclusions, a caution which at times seems very exasperating to the student or layman.

If this kind of three-variable situation could be used as a realistic model, life would be relatively simple for the social scientist. But unfortunately there will be a number of complications which tend to introduce further ambiguities into the situation and which create a need for a much more technical knowledge of methodology. Let me indicate briefly what a few of these complications are in order to illustrate the need for highly quantitative research.

Some Complications

ALTERNATIVE MODELS

Even in the three-variable case, there is an alternative model or explanation that can account equally well for the same empirical data given in the above tables. Instead of causing both X and Y, Z may be an intervening causal link between them. That is, X may cause Z, which in turn causes Y (i.e., $X \rightarrow Z \rightarrow Y$). Common sense would again suggest that since Z stands between X and Y in a causal sequence, it should be more highly correlated with both X and Y than X and Y are with each other. It can be shown more rigorously that if other causal factors have a net or aggregate random effect, then in this situation, as well as the previous one, a control for Z will wipe out the relationship between X and Y. We thus see that there are several alternative models—involving the same variables—that explain the facts equally well. In this case, perhaps, religious preference affects one's occupation (say, through motivational factors), which in turn affects political preference. According to this interpretation, religion is an indirect cause of political preference, and we would reach a very different practical and theoretical conclusion from that implied by the first model.

In general, there will always be more than one explanation for each set of data, and it will be necessary to use supplementary information to choose among them. In our example we have used only correlations or associations, having said nothing at all about temporal sequences. If we knew that religious factors preceded the choice of occupation, then this information could be used to rule out the first (spurious model) situation in favor of the second. On the other hand, if respondents changed their religious preferences after selecting their occupations, then we might decide in favor of the first alternative. That is, if we know time sequences as well as correlations, we are in a better position to choose among alternative explanations. This fact has important implications for research design, since it implies that, whenever possible, we should collect data at more than one point in time.

ADDITIONAL VARIABLES

A second kind of complication arises if there are two (or more) sources of spuriousness, as indicated in the following diagram:

For example, the relationship between religion and political preference may be due to two common causes, occupation and region of the country (which is often a surrogate for numerous other factors). One section of the country may be heavily Protestant and Republican. It would then be necessary to control *simultaneously* for region and occupation. In this very simple example, such control could be accomplished by setting up a series of tables, one for white-collar workers in the South, one for blue-collar workers in the South, one for white-collar workers in the Northeast, and so forth. If there were five regions and two occupational levels, this would necessitate ten separate tables, each of which related religion to political preference.

This principle can be readily extended to any number of control variables. If there were four separate sources of spuriousness (say occupation, region, sex, and race), then in order to hold all of these constant at once there would have to be a separate table for each combination of the control factors (e.g., one table including only white, Southern, blue-collar males; a second including only white, Southern, blue-collar females, and so forth). As can easily be imagined, this process of controlling becomes cumbersome and difficult for a reader to follow. But more important, a point will be reached where there are insufficient numbers of cases in each table. For example, with five regions, two races, two sexes, and two occupational levels there would have to be forty separate tables. With only two hundred cases to begin with, this would mean an average of only five cases per table. One very important implication is that if one suspects that a large number of controls will be needed, he will have to begin with a very large sample. Fortunately, there are alternative (more complex) ways of controlling for many variables at once, but these also involve certain kinds of simplifying assumptions. If reality is complex, so must be the analysis!

CORRELATED INDEPENDENT VARIABLES

A third kind of complication occurs in situations such as that described in the introductory chapter, where a number of the variables thought to be causally related to the dependent variable are themselves highly intercorrelated. For example, in the case of the poverty syndrome of low education, low income, unemployment, broken families, and low aspirations— all of which might be possible sources of high crime rates— how can the separate effects of each variable be inferred?

Recall that the major advantage of experimental designs was that several causal factors may be independently manipulated so that their effects are not confounded together. But in the real world they *are* found together. Of course their intercorrelations will not be perfect. There are some people with poor educations having high incomes; some unemployed fathers may instill high aspirations in their children. This fact makes it possible to separate out their individual effects provided samples are very large and provided very good measures can be obtained for each variable. But it necessitates a much more complex kind of statistical analysis. Given the limitations of any particular research project, it is often impossible to separate the component effects of individual variables with any degree of confidence. In these instances, they must be treated as a single "syndrome," or as a cluster of variables that must be considered all at once.

MEASUREMENT ERRORS

A fourth kind of complication is introduced by the presence of measurement errors, which in the social sciences are often quite large. As already implied, the more highly intercorrelated the causal variables, the more serious the distortions produced by measurement errors. In effect, measurement errors introduce additional unknowns into the testing situation, and where measurement errors are unknown (or undetected), the distortions may be very serious. In simple situations one can state what kinds of effects particular kinds of measurement errors will have. For example, in the first (spurious) causal situation we examined, where Z is a common cause of both X and Y, it can be shown that if there is random measurement error in Z, then the relationship between X and Y will *not* reduce to zero if Z is controlled. In effect, it will be imperfectly controlled because of the fact that the investigator will not know the true values of Z.

This problem of evaluating the effects of measurement error is highly complex, but the implications are clear. Really definitive studies designed to sort out component causes in complex situations cannot be made until measurement problems have been resolved. Thus in a very real sense the advancement of any science depends on the adequacy of its measurement procedures.

INTERACTION EFFECTS

The possibility of interaction effects of peculiar combinations constitutes a fifth kind of complication. As simple first approximations, the effects of several variables may be taken to be additive. These additive effects are the "main effects" discussed in connection with experimental designs. For example, if we are trying to explain a person's income, we might begin by adding the effects of education, sex, and race. That is, there may be a constant increment, say $2,000, "added" to one's income for being a male, and another constant for being white, over and above the expected amount given one's educational attainment. We could write income I as a simple sum of the effects of education E, sex S, and race R. Thus

$$I = E + S + R$$

where we would need to fill in the proper constants in front of each variable on the right-hand side.

But what if there were relatively small differences between the incomes of whites and nonwhites at low educational levels but rather large ones at the higher levels? Or what if the differences between the incomes of white and nonwhite women were much less than those for the men? Or what if education made a bigger difference for the incomes of men than for women? Then this very simple kind of additive model would not work, and we would have an example of interaction. We could not speak simply of *the* relationship between education and income; we would need to qualify our statement by referring specifically to the sex and race of the individuals concerned.

In effect, we might have four different relationships, one each for white males, nonwhite males, white females, and nonwhite females. The relationships in this case would be much more complex, and our explanations of them would also have to be more complex. Hypothetically the relationships might look something like those given in Figure 4. Had the relationship been a simple additive one, the result could have been represented by a series of *parallel* curves, as indicated in Figure 5. When the curves are parallel, there is always a constant difference or increment between any two curves, say those for white and nonwhite males.

RECIPROCAL CAUSATION

The sixth and final kind of complication arises whenever there is reciprocal causation, or two-way influences, among some of the variables. In real-life situations we recognize that this occurs very frequently, though often with a time lag involved. In our poverty example we assume that low levels of educa-

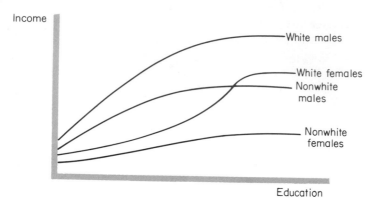

Figure 4

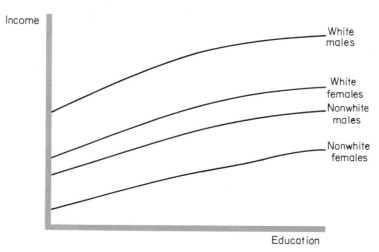

Figure 5

tion, occupation, and income of one generation produce low motivation and numerous school dropouts in the next generation, which in turn affect the jobs and income the second generation will receive, and so on through successive generations. It would not be particularly difficult to handle this kind of situation analytically, but practically speaking one cannot draw neat generational distinctions when aggregate populations are concerned. Exactly who is in what generation? There will be a continuous distribution of ages, and therefore it is only within individual families that one can speak in terms of distinct generations.

Whenever we allow for the possibility of reciprocal causation, whereby X can affect Y and Y also affect X, we encounter a fundamental difficulty that shows up in the mathematical equations as a situation where there will be too many unknowns, none of which can be estimated from the data alone. On the more common-sense level, the difficulty boils down to the question of deciding whether X has a bigger impact on Y or Y a bigger impact on X—a kind of chicken-egg problem.

The resolution to this kind of problem requires complex estimation procedures that have been developed by statisticians and economists. To oversimplify considerably, there seem to be two possible ways to resolve the chicken-egg problem created by this kind of situation. The first is to collect what are called time-series data, that is, data on the same individuals over a reasonably prolonged period of time. Economists are fortunate in that income, cost, and production data are available to them on a regular basis. Furthermore, these data are reasonably well standardized across industries since many items can be compared in terms of dollars (e.g., labor costs or sales prices) or easily counted (e.g., number of automobiles produced). Time-series data can also be gathered in small-group experiments. For example, the observer may take a frequency count of aggressive acts every fifteen minutes, or the group may be measured during regular weekly meetings. But many kinds of data are expensive to collect, and most individuals will object to being asked the same questions over and over again. Panel studies, in which the same respondent is interviewed perhaps three times, would seem to be about the best we can hope for in survey research.

The second kind of resolution involves finding additional causes of the reciprocally related variables that are not themselves in any way dependent on these variables. A favorite example cited by economists is rainfall. Wheat yields, and therefore prices, are clearly dependent on rainfall, but rainfall is not dependent on any economic variables. A problem even with this example is that as humans gain increasing control over their environment, there will be fewer and fewer of these truly independent variables. It may not be too long before rainfall becomes dependent on the farmer's behavior.

Not only must one locate such truly independent variables, but he must make certain *a priori* (usually untestable) assumptions about which of these independent variables cause specific dependent variables. He must not allow for the possibility that every independent variable affects every dependent variable directly, or he will be back in the same situation of having too many unknowns. He must introduce these additional independent variables *selectively* in order to be in a position to resolve the chicken-egg problem. For example, the economist assumes that rainfall affects agricultural yields and therefore the supply of these goods, but he assumes that it does not directly affect customers' tastes or preferences for these goods. If this assumption were unrealistic, he would have to find some other causal variable to do the job.

This completes our very brief summary of certain kinds of complicating factors that make inferences difficult in non-experimental research. The impression I wish to convey is that the resolution of these complications is not at all simple, cannot depend on common sense, tricks of the trade, or "intuition," and will ultimately require large-scale and expensive research. Much has already been learned about the nature of the methodological issues involved. That is, we know what many of the problems are and the technical conditions that must be met in order to resolve them. But there are many practical difficulties standing in our way, and we cannot expect any dramatic "breakthroughs" of the kinds that have occurred in physics or chemistry.

The Development of Systematic Theory

In view of all this complexity and the literally thousands of topics with which the social scientist may deal, how can we possibly develop reasonable guidelines for selecting among numerous variables and problems? Is there any hope that an extremely large number of miscellaneous facts can be integrated into a small number of rather coherent bundles? Social scientists are well aware of the need for sound theory that will integrate research findings, provide the necessary guidelines, and make comparative analyses more simple. But it seems fair to say that we are not very far along the road to achieving this objective.

Let me speak primarily in terms of sociology for the remainder of this chapter. There have been a number of "grand theorists," the latest and most prominent of whom is Talcott Parsons of Harvard, who have attempted to make major inroads into the difficult problem of integrating the field theoretically. Researchers have generally found, however, that the primary value of these theories has been in providing what have been termed "sensitizing concepts" which alert the investigator to the possible importance of a given set of variables. For example, we have the concept of "role," which sensitizes the sociologist to look for certain regularized patterns of behavior that are relatively independent of the particular individuals who happen to be occupying the positions and performing the role obligations. But the grand theorists have provided us with relatively few specific *propositions* that are sufficiently precise to yield testable hypotheses.

Robert Merton, one of Parsons' students, was one of the first sociologists to make explicit the position—now probably endorsed by the overwhelming majority of sociologists—that our greatest need is for theories of the "middle range." [2] I would interpret this to mean theories that attempt to explain particular kinds of phenomena with sufficient clarity and concreteness to imply a set of interrelated hypotheses that can be applied to several apparently diverse phenomena. We have a number of theoretical discussions of large-scale organizations and bureaucratic behavior that are meant to account for patterns in many different kinds of such organizations: business firms, labor unions, political parties, prisons, churches, and so forth. Yet they are not designed to account for all human behavior, international conflict, or societal development. Their

[2] This point of view is elaborated in Robert K. Merton, *Social Theory and Social Structure* (New York: The Free Press of Glencoe, 1957, rev. ed.), Chaps. 1–3.

objectives and limitations are relatively narrow, and their propositions are reasonably specific.

One of the greatest needs in sociological theory is for middle-range theories that can suggest, in very specific ways, how findings about particular phenomena can be used to shed light on other phenomena. There are thousands of different forms of "deviance," only a few of which are socially defined as serious enough to come to the attention of the public—crime, suicide, drug addiction, overt rebellion, and so forth. Suppose the social scientist studying burglary had to develop a theory of burglary completely independently of a theory used to account for homicide. Given the large number of explanatory variables that might be used in each case, this would be an extremely wasteful procedure. It would be preferable to have a theory that accounted for both burglary and homicide and that also explained suicide as well. In fact, it would be desirable to have an explanation for all forms of deviance.

But while such a general theory might be desirable, it may not be realistic to suppose that it would at the same time be adequate for explaining all forms of deviance, just as a theoretical explanation for "disease" would be of little value to the practicing physician. One runs the risk that an extremely general explanation, if in fact "true," will be so vague or abstract that it will not make any really specific predictions capable of being tested by empirical research. For example, one might explain all deviance in terms of parental rejection or "strains" that have been produced in the individual. But such theories rarely specify the mechanisms producing one form of deviance rather than another, nor do they account for varying degrees of deviance. What they do accomplish is a sensitizing function. They may suggest that the investigator look for strains or parental rejection as a first step in his analysis.

Many such very general explanations have a good deal of popular appeal because of their simplicity and programmatic nature. All we need to do to prevent deviance is to reduce the strains and get parents to behave better! And being vague, these theories can be used to account ex post facto for almost any form of deviance that may occur. They may be modified, elaborated, and made seemingly more technical as the occasion demands. But their predictive power may be very weak. The problem is therefore that of making them more specific by spelling out very explicitly what they imply under carefully defined conditions. In effect, this will produce a number of "subtheories" of the middle range.

Thus in any science there is a strain between the need for relatively simple general explanations on the one hand and more specific theories of a narrower range of applicability on the other. There will also be differences of opinion regarding priorities as to how these should be developed. Perhaps most social scientists would agree that both are needed and that each supports the other, but there will be much less consensus regarding how much time and energy should be devoted to each. In sociology much more energy is presently being devoted to the more specific formulations, leaving a considerable distance between our most general theories and the actual research being conducted in the field.

Why not dispense with theories and simply get down to earth? Why not select some concrete problem, such as urban slum life or the Viet Nam war, and design studies to shed light on these problems? In short, why not deal primarily with our important social problems as they arise? This is certainly an important kind of criticism of current social science research, and it must be answered. One answer can be given in terms of knowledge for its own sake. The scientist is not concerned with how his theories and findings are to be applied. He is basically an intellectual whose curiosity has been aroused, and our aesthetic appreciation of his work ought to be sufficient justification in and of itself.

While I think there is much to be said for this position, I do not believe that it would appeal to most students or laymen nor even to many scientists themselves. We have seen too many examples of scientists producing weapons of destruction, and of, in effect, selling themselves to the highest bidder, to give credence to the naive assumption that, in the long run, scientific advances will necessarily work toward the benefit of mankind. Social scientists, in particular, are sensitive to this kind of problem. They see billions being spent on rocket research while people are starving and discrimination is producing serious social problems. Yet most social scientists seem to believe that basic or nonapplied research is absolutely essential, even where the ultimate objective is to shed light on practical problems of the day. Why should this be the case?

The difficulty with purely applied research and attention to current practical problems is that the problems change much more rapidly than our ability to study them. By the time we had conducted a thorough study of one phenomenon, it might have given way to another. In fact, activists argue that "research" is often used as an excuse for doing nothing. What they seem to mean is that it will take so long to conduct the research that the problem will have either disappeared or been obscured or forgotten. This is sometimes true and must be freely admitted. Even if the phenomenon has not changed completely, many of the specifics may change with sufficient rapidity that by the time the research report has been made available the findings will no longer accurately describe the true state of affairs. For example, the study may report that 53 per cent of whites favor school integration, but a series of riots that have intervened between the time of the interviews and the time of the report may have shifted the true percentage downward to 20 per cent. An action policy based on this dated finding might fail because of its inaccuracy.

Scientific theories cannot consist of such dated relationships, except as admissions of one's ignorance of the true causal mechanisms. Astronomical laws that merely described the positions of specific bodies, say the planets of the solar system, would not be very useful unless these positions were repeated with a high degree of regularity. Astronomers are fortunate that such a high degree of regularity does in fact occur, though for many phenomena they study (such as the movement of distant stars) the movement is so imperceptible, relative to the times between observations, that other kinds of laws would be necessary to predict their long-run behavior. The fact that such extreme regularities do not occur in the social realm has led many observers to the pessimistic conclusion that the scientific study of human beings is impossible.

The most useful scientific laws, then, are those that do not refer directly to concrete events (e.g., the position of Venus at 8:05 P.M., July 1, 1970) but are instead phrased more generally in the form of "if-then" statements. *If* a body is moving with a particular velocity and momentum in a specified gravitational field, *then* its position can be expected to change according to some specified law. If one then wants to refer to a particular historical event, such as the position of Venus on a given day, this general law can be applied to the concrete case. In addition to the law itself, however, it will be necessary to supply some concrete facts about the mass and present velocity of Venus and its present position in relation to the sun and other planets. It will also be necessary to make certain simplifying assumptions about the lack of disturbances from outside factors (e.g., nearby stars).

This example illustrates the important point that a precisely formulated general law, plus some assumptions about neglected factors, plus a set of facts that are peculiar to some particular phenomenon, may actually be used to forecast what will happen. In the absence of the law, a less satisfactory forecast may be made by merely extrapolating past and present behavior into the future. This latter kind of forecast may in fact be a very good one, provided there are no important changes in any of the variables. One might take the number of urban riots in the summers of 1965, 1966, and 1967 and obtain an estimate five years into the future under the assumption that, whatever the causes of the riots, they will continue to operate as they have before. This, of course, gives us no insights as to how the number of riots may be reduced or how the fundamental causes may be discerned and manipulated.

One of the most serious and difficult problems confronting the social scientist is that of developing reasonably general laws of social behavior that are not so restricted as to time and place that they can be applied only under very limited circumstances. The more restrictive the law, the less likely that it will remain appropriate for use in practical situations, which means that its implications cannot be continually tested. Even if a general theory of "hippie" behavior could be constructed and tested, and even if it predicted hippie behavior extremely well, its usefulness would disappear with the last hippie colony. Perhaps a variation of the hippie theme might later appear, in which case the theory might again be applied with minor modifications, but clearly a theory restricted to this single kind of deviant behavior will be useful only to the extent that the phenomenon continues to persist. The theory would be much more useful if it could be generalized to include, let us say, all forms of "escapist" deviance. But such a more general formulation would undoubtedly be less specific regarding details, and its predictions would be much less precise.

Thus we have a peculiar kind of dilemma in many of the social sciences owing to the fact that the phenomena we study are often not as persistent and regular—relative to the time it takes to study them—as in some of the physical sciences. Yet many social phenomena appear to be all too persistent: wars, prejudice and discrimination, crime, and many kinds of interpersonal conflict. Many less "problematic" phenomena are also persistent: the formation of friendship cliques, authority relationships within bureaucratic organizations, socialization patterns within the family, and the like. It would seem possible to develop reasonably specific theories of these phenomena, even in the absence of highly general laws that are relatively timeless. But in the case of the more fleeting phenomena, we may have to rely on much more general theories with less specific predictive value.

If reasonably general laws of human behavior are to be found, they will undoubtedly have to be fairly complex if they are to be applied to a wide range of specific phenomena. For example, simple statements of the form, "the greater the X, the greater the Y," will have to be modified by spelling out the conditions under which they can be applied. A good deal of attention must also be given to the question of exactly what is to be included as an X or a Y.

Let me illustrate in terms of dominance-subordinance relationships. It would certainly be useful if we could explain many different forms of dominance relationships in terms of a single theory of power. For example, what is there in common in the parent-child, white-black, citizen-criminal, and large nation-small nation relationships? Can we spell out the conditions under which increasing punishment by the dominant party will lead to increased resistance by the subordinate party, as contrasted with the conditions under which the subordinate party will yield? If a really adequate theory existed, then it would be possible to apply it to some new power relationship not yet systematically studied (e.g., power relationships between college administrations and student rebels).

But as the theory is made more general, the concepts or variables in that theory become much more abstract and difficult to measure. It may not be too difficult to spell out a set of conditions that affect relationships between whites and blacks in the United States in the 1960's, but can our conceptualization of these conditions be broadened so that they have something in common with the conditions that affect relationships among nations or between husbands and wives? Are there any general methodological principles that can be applied so as to provide useful guidelines for this generalization process? Philosophers of science have given a good deal of thought to this kind of question on a very abstract level, but there seem to be very few really useful guidelines that the practicing social scientist can use in constructing specific theories and then moving in some systematic way to explanations of a more general nature.

One of the reasons for the difficulty here is that there are fundamental problems of measurement involved. Can one measure prejudice toward blacks, women, or Communists in such a way that it is reasonable to conclude that they are all tapping the same kind of general attitude? Can the term "punishment" be conceptualized and measured so that it applies to nations punishing each other as well as to parents punishing children? We shall consider such measurement problems in the next chapter, where we shall see that the processes of measurement and theory construction are intimately interrelated.

5

Measurement

Why is measurement of crucial importance to the development of the social sciences? In part, the answers have already been implied in the previous discussion, but it is now necessary to be much more specific. Critics of the quantitative approach to social research have often claimed that social scientists are merely obsessed by the need to be "scientific" and to win respect among academics as being hard-nosed and objective rather than speculative and highly subjective. When I first became interested in sociology as a professional career, this was exactly my own reaction. It seemed to me that social scientists were spending too much time talking about the necessity of being scientific and of improving their measurements but that in fact they were doing very little about it. I have now come to see, however, that problems of measurement are much more complex than I originally realized. In this chapter I shall try to indicate what some of these basic complexities seem to be and how social scientists are attempting to resolve them.

One reason why accurate measurement is necessary has been suggested in the previous chapter. If the supposed causes of a phenomenon such as delinquency or discrimination are highly intercorrelated, it becomes technically impossible to separate out their component effects without accurate measures. In general, the more highly interrelated they are, the more accurate our measures of each must be. But even where we have correctly identified and isolated one or two important variables, accurate measurement may be necessary in order to refine the analysis beyond the common-sense level. For example, we commonly hear the assertion that the more nonwhites there are in an area, the greater the discrimination. But does this imply a straight-line or linear relationship between a particular kind of discrimination and minority percentage? Or is a curvilinear relationship more appropriate? If so, then exactly what kind of a curve will work best? Obviously the better our measurement of both variables, the more precise we can be about exact forms of relationships. Perhaps the curves will vary with respect to form according to the type of community or presence of other minorities. If so, precise measurement will enable the investigator to learn more about the conditions affecting the relationship.

To these important reasons why measurement needs to be improved, we can add at least one more. Measurement considerations often enable us to clarify our theoretical thinking and to suggest new variables that should be considered. It is often thought, prior to actual attempts at measurement, that we really understand the nature of a phenomenon because we have experienced it directly. For instance, it might be assumed that everyone has a basic understanding of what "prejudice" is. But as soon as someone begins to measure it, the claim will inevitably arise that true prejudice cannot "really" be measured by any paper-and-pencil test. Its "true essence" cannot be captured. If the hypothetical critic is questioned as to exactly what this "true essence" is, however, he will usually find it almost impossible to convey exactly what he means. He may construct his own paper-and-pencil test, in which case an argument is likely to occur as to which test is the "best" measure of prejudice, the essence of which is thought to be understood.

This is how science must proceed. When one attempts to spell out the specific procedures to be used in the measurement process (e.g., the specific questions he will ask), it may be discovered that different persons had basically different conceptions as to what a notion such as "prejudice" is meant to convey. As data are actually collected, it may also be found that responses to the questions do not hang together as had originally been expected. For example whites who tend to use unfavorable stereotypes of blacks (e.g., dirty, lazy, or aggressive) may not necessarily be the ones who would prefer to avoid them. In effect, the data may lead one to infer several distinct dimensions of prejudice that are not very highly intercorrelated. This in turn means that prejudice should not be studied as though it were a single variable. There may be different kinds of prejudice that have very different implications for theories of discrimination. In fact, this turns out to be the case. The important general point is that careful attention to measurement may force a clarification of one's basic concepts and theories.

The Indirectness of Measurement

Perhaps the most frequently encountered objection to efforts at precise measurement in the social sciences resolves down to the argument that such measurement is often highly indirect. As we shall see, *all* measurement is to some degree indirect, even in physics, the most precise science with which the social sciences can be compared. But while social scientists can readily point to this fact and argue by analogy that their problems are basically no different from those of physical scientists, it seems only realistic to admit that the difficulty is an important one. In order to illustrate its generality, while at the same time indicating some special difficulties facing the social scientist, I shall begin by briefly considering a simple kind of measurement problem in physics.

Even on the intuitive level, we have learned to think of the "mass" of a body in terms of some kind of postulated property involving a quantity of matter. Yet the measurement of mass is not as direct as we sometimes suppose. Basically, the measurement of such quantities as mass (or length, or time) involves obtaining pointer readings under standardized conditions and then inferring a body's mass on the basis of such pointer readings. We may construct a causal interpretation of the measurement process, in this case, somewhat as follows. The actual pointer reading one obtains from the scale is determined by a number of factors, only one of which is the presumed mass of the body. If a spring scale is being used, the pointer reading is determined by (a) the mass of the body, (b) the gravitational force of the earth, (c) properties of the scale itself (e.g., properties of the metal spring), (d) properties of the scientist who reads the scale, and (e) numerous miscellaneous factors, no one of which has any major significance.

How, then, do we infer "mass" from the pointer reading? In effect, we do so by making more or less realistic assumptions about the other variables that possibly affect the readings. Sometimes these assumptions can be made on the basis of theory or well established "fact." In this example the gravitational force of the earth is assumed to be known, and adjustments can be made for any departures from sea level. We recognize a certain circularity in this kind of theoretical argument, since somewhere some theoretical assumptions must have been made in order to find a starting point. This illustrates the general observation that the existence of an adequate theory may aid in the measurement process. Here it might reasonably be assumed that the effects of the earth's gravitational pull are constant from one replication to the next, so that any differences in pointer readings could not be attributed to this particular factor.

Properties of the scale itself, such as the quality of the metal spring, might also account for the pointer readings. It is usually assumed that the measuring instrument possesses certain constant properties and that it has been well calibrated by comparing the pointer readings using this particular weighing scale with those using other standardized scales. Again, there is a certain circularity in the argument. How does one know that the properties of the standard scale are really constant? Perhaps all such scales have changing properties known only to a mysterious demon who manipulates these properties so that they all change in the same way. We simply make the rather plausible assumption that this is not the case and that the properties of the measuring instrument can be taken as constant over the period of observation. Thus we must not only make theoretical assumptions, but we must also make assumptions about our measuring instruments.

There are also the varying properties of the observer himself and of countless minor disturbances. Recognizing, for example, that any human observer's judgment regarding the coincidence of a pointer with a given line will depend on the condition of his eyes and numerous psychological factors, the physicist relies on mechanical or electronic substitutes in so far as possible. As a final caution, he insists on *repeated* measurements or replication in order to cancel out the effects of random disturbances. Ultimately, then, he can only make probability statements that in effect depend upon the assumption that disturbances are operating in accord with known laws of probability. If they are in fact operating in some unknown systematic manner, he may obtain biased measures, and any inferences based on these measures may be faulty.

Exactly the same principles apply to measurement in the social sciences, but it is unfortunately much more difficult to make realistic assumptions about disturbances. This is due to a combination of reasons. First, we lack the well grounded theories that might be used to specify other forces (e.g., gravity) that might be operative. Second, we cannot be so easily assured that our measuring instruments are well calibrated against an objective standard or that they possess constant properties. This means that if we get different results from one replication to the next, it will be difficult to separate out real changes from those resulting from the measurement process itself. Finally, there are a number of practical reasons why repeated measurements are both more difficult and less useful in the case of human subjects.

Therefore, while we may legitimately claim that the basic problems of measurement are similar from one science to the next, this very simple kind of assertion can mask a number of very real difficulties that the social scientist must face because of the fact that all measurement is necessarily indirect. "Indirect-ness" is a matter of degree, and in general the more indirect the measurement the larger the number of untested assumptions that must be strung together in order to make valid tests of one's theory.

In order to make this rather general point much more spe-cific, I shall turn next to the very intriguing problem of attitude measurement. Are there any reasonably rigorous ways of infer-ring what is going on inside a person's head by examining the patterning of his responses to paper-and-pencil tests? How and why is this problem more complex than that of inferring the properties of a body (e.g., its mass) on the basis of its behavior when placed on a scale? Are human beings so variable, or so whimsical, that the task is virtually hopeless? Are there ways of obtaining repeated measures without at the same time changing the person being studied?

Attitude Measurement [1]

Suppose an investigator wishes to test the hypothesis that the greater a person's political conservatism, the greater his preju-dice toward minorities. It will obviously be necessary to mea-sure both prejudice and political conservatism, neither of which may have been very clearly defined. Even if rather specific definitions have been given to both concepts, it will still be necessary to come to grips with a number of important problems in the process of actually constructing a set of questions de-signed to measure each variable.

One basic decision that must be made concerns the level of generality on which the hypothesis is to be tested. Is the concern

[1] There is an extensive literature on attitude measurement, much of which is fairly technical. A good place to begin is with general texts on research methods. See especially Selltiz *et al.*, *Research Methods in Social Relations* (New York: Holt, Rinehart & Winston, 1959) and William J. Goode and Paul K. Hatt, *Methods in Social Research* (New York: McGraw-Hill Book Co., 1952).

with prejudice toward all minorities or just toward blacks? What kinds of areas of political conservatism are to be tapped? Economic conservatism? Conservatism with respect to civil liberties? International relations? And how specific should the items be? Should they refer to a particular bill presently before the Congress? To school desegregation? To the role of the United States in Viet Nam?

The basic dilemma in this connection is that, on the one hand, specific questions are often necessary in order to make the items relevant to the respondent. He may have definite ideas regarding our role in Viet Nam or school integration, yet he may respond in the socially approved manner to some general question about the abstract rights of minorities or the right of individuals to a fair trial. On the other hand, if questions are made too specific, they immediately become dated and of very little general interest. If someone wished to replicate the study five years later, both Viet Nam and school desegregation might have become dead issues. Nor could the study be replicated in other countries with any expectation that the same kinds of variables were being tapped. Naturally a Frenchman might disapprove of the intervention of the United States in Viet Nam while similarly endorsing integration in the United States, but this might tell us very little about his general level of prejudice or his political conservatism. One would have to find a different set of items more relevant to French affairs.

Thus the objective of finding measurement instruments that are sensitive enough to distinguish among different levels of a variable, such as prejudice, may require the use of highly specific items. But this conflicts with the aim of developing measures that are sufficiently general to be applied to a wide variety of contexts and over a reasonable period of time. Even in the case of very general questions, the possibility exists that they will have different meanings to various persons. A skeptic can always claim that they may be tapping a different underlying motive or attitude in different contexts. One answer to such a skeptic is to disclaim any intention of inferring anything beyond the actual responses to the questions. That is, one may say that he is not really interested in the underlying attitudes but merely in the responses themselves. But why select a particular set of perhaps ten questions out of literally thousands that might have been asked? This kind of answer to the skeptic is obviously unsatisfactory.

A second kind of decision that must always be made concerns the degree to which the purposes of the measurement should be disguised. How do we know that the respondents will tell us how they really feel and think? Perhaps they will merely tell us what they think we want to hear or what they consider to be the socially approved answer. There seem to be two basic ways to resolve this kind of difficulty. The first is to make no effort to disguise the fact that the questions are designed to get at prejudice, conservatism, or some other controversial topic, but to assure the respondent that it is to his advantage to be perfectly candid. If this approach is used, the interviewer must go to great lengths to achieve good rapport with the respondent and to assure him that he will remain anonymous and that there is no possible way that his answers can hurt him. In addition, an appeal can be made that the respondent is representing other people like him (which is true) and that the investigator needs to know what he really thinks. As previously noted, once such rapport and trust have been established, most respondents are willing to talk freely about very controversial subjects, and it is then assumed that no systematic biases have been introduced. In a few instances it is possible to build in cross-checks by asking essentially the same question in several different ways, but a clever respondent could fool the investigator if he so desired. The essential objective, of course, is to make him realize that there is no reason why he should need to do this.

But perhaps the respondent is only fooling himself! The above strategy presupposes that the respondent is a rational individual who is conscious of his true attitudes and who also has a rather definite opinion about most of the questions that are being asked. What if these assumptions are false? Or what if the respondent recognizes his prejudice but guards it carefully against all intruders, even the most friendly and reassuring interviewer? Or what if the subject is so controversial that very few respondents can be expected to cooperate? A second general strategy can then be used. This second approach depends on the assumption that if the true purpose of the study can be carefully disguised, the respondent's underlying motives and attitudes can be inferred by the skillful analysis of his responses to very vague stimuli that elicit open-ended answers. For example, he may be shown a set of pictures, some of which involve both blacks and whites, and may be asked to tell a story about each of them. His prejudice is then inferred by a study of the stories he writes. Or his conservatism might be inferred from his responses to a set of items, none of which directly refers to politics, economics, or international relations, but perhaps to hypothetical relations with parents, children, religious authorities, and so forth.

The difficulty with these "projective" techniques, as they are called, is that the measurement becomes much more indirect and open to various interpretations. In short, the biases of the investigator may very well intrude. One person reading the stories of the respondent may "see" a large amount of disguised hostility toward minorities, whereas a second reader may not. In effect, the interpretations of the stories may tell more about the reader-investigator than they do about the respondents! In order to avoid this difficulty, social scientists who use such projective techniques have developed rather elaborate and standardized ways of scoring the stories or other kinds of responses. Only well trained scorers seem capable of reaching a high degree of agreement on how to score each respondent, and there is always the nagging question as to how much disagreement there would be among scorers trained in very different settings.

Again, the skeptic can always claim that the "true essence" of the attitude in question is not being tapped or that, in spite of all of the efforts to disguise the purpose, the respondents were actually covering up their true sentiments. As we have seen throughout the previous chapters, there are many places where an unreasonable skeptic may fault *any* study, no matter how carefully designed it has been. This is especially the case where one is concerned with the measurement of attitudes. Our task is therefore that of convincing the reasonable skeptic that a large number of precautions have been taken and that others might have been taken had it not been for limitations of time, money, or existing knowledge.

For the remainder of this section I would like to focus on one of the most challenging problems confronting the student of attitude measurement. How does one tell whether the questions being used are tapping a single basic attitude or several different ones at the same time? Put another way, are there several different dimensions being tapped, or is it realistic to assume that individuals can be ranked along a single continuum from high to low, favorable to unfavorable, or liberal to conservative?

I believe it has been historically true that in most cases where investigators have studied what they thought to be a single dimension (say, prejudice or political conservatism) they have later inferred that two or more distinct dimensions were involved. This kind of discovery may result in considerable refinement over common sense. For example, it has been found that political conservatism seems to have at least two very distinct dimensions. Persons who are liberal with respect to economic issues (e.g., favorableness toward unions or social security) may or may not be liberal with respect to civil liberties and minority rights. Therefore the simple distinction between "liberals" and "conservatives" may be highly misleading, both practically and theoretically.

The use of simple scoring procedures may actually make it impossible to study the possibility that a given set of questions may be tapping more than one attitude dimension. In effect, they may force an ordering on the data, so that individuals are automatically ranked from high to low regardless of how the patterns of responses come out. This can be illustrated in terms of a very common kind of attitude scale constructed by merely adding the scores for each separate question.

Suppose the respondent has been given a set of items to which he is asked to indicate whether he "strongly agrees," "agrees," is neutral or has no opinion, "disagrees," or "strongly disagrees." Scores may then be assigned to his responses by some arbitrary system (say, scoring the above responses as 5, 4, 3, 2, and 1 respectively). This is done for each of the questions and a total score obtained. Some of the questions will be worded oppositely, so that an "agree" answer indicates high prejudice on one item, whereas a "disagree" indicates high prejudice on the next item, but this can easily be handled by reversing the scores on (say) the second item.

For example, two statements might be:

1. Blacks and whites should attend separate schools.
2. Blacks should be given exactly the same political rights as whites.

Scores might be constructed so that high scores indicate high prejudice. In the above example a person who "strongly agrees" with the first statement and "disagrees" with the second might receive a score of 5 on the first question and 4 on the second; someone who "disagrees" with the first and who is neutral on the second would receive scores of 2 and 3 on the respective items.

It can readily be seen that, since everyone will receive some numerical total score, a simple adding of the scores will result in the automatic ranking of all individuals regardless of what items happened to be used. In fact, one could readily construct a nonsense "scale" consisting, let us say, of ten disconnected questions. In such a case, most people's scores would come out somewhere near the middle of the possible range, but just by chance some might receive scores near the maximum or minimum. They could then be ranked along the "dimension" concerned. It is in this sense that we can say that the method forces an ordering on the data. If the items in fact all tap a single attitudinal dimension, then all is well. But if they do not, then the result is likely to be a nonsense conclusion, if it could be recognized as such, or—much worse—a misleading conclusion.

FACTOR ANALYSIS

One rather obvious way around this particular difficulty is to study the individual questions to see whether they hang together properly. Presumably, if they are all tapping the same thing, say prejudice, then the items ought to be correlated with each other. That is, if a person answers in a prejudiced manner to one question, he is relatively more likely to answer in a prejudiced way to the other questions. Obviously, we do not expect perfect relationships, since each question will have its idiosyncratic aspects for any given individual. One person who is generally very prejudiced may have had several pleasant contacts with Negroes in athletics and may not object to integrated sports. A second may have strong opinions about minority political rights because his father stressed this position. Because of the fact that each individual question has its idiosyncratic aspects, which can be thought of as producing random measurement error, it is usually desirable to use at least five or six items. In effect, this is one of the social scientist's forms of replication. In studying how well the questions hang together, the social scientist is essentially trying to decide the degree to which his replications all involve measures of the same thing.

In general, the less directly related the questions are to the specific attitude being studied, the less highly correlated we would expect them to be with each other and the more opportunity arises for random noise to operate. But this is not necessarily the case, since a number of items might be tapping some other attitudinal dimension not explicitly taken into consideration. It therefore becomes necessary to study the *patterns* of intercorrelations among items, as well as their absolute magnitudes. But as soon as we admit this kind of difficulty, simple common-sense rules of thumb cannot be used. Let us consider a specific example in order to illustrate the point.

Suppose an investigator measures political conservatism by using twelve questions, four of which tap economic conservatism, four deal with civil liberties, and four with international relations. Suppose, also, that in reality each of these three dimensions of conservatism are completely unrelated to each other. In other words, if we knew that a person is economically conservative, this would tell us absolutely nothing about either his attitudes concerning civil liberties or those dealing with international issues.

In this case people who are economically conservative are no more (or less) likely to be liberal with respect to civil liber-

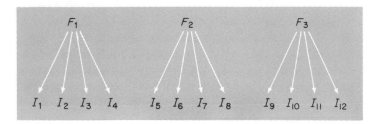

Figure 6

ties than are those who are liberal on economic issues. This situation could be diagramed as in Figure 6, in which the three distinct dimensions of political conservatism have been designated as F_1, F_2, and F_3, and where the items have been designated as I_1, I_2, ..., I_{12}. The underlying attitudinal dimensions represented by the F's are referred to as "factors" and the responses to the twelve questions as "indicators" of these factors (hence the designations F and I).

In the diagram of Figure 6, items 1–4 are indicators of F_1, which we are taking to be economic conservatism; items 5–8 are indicators of F_2 (civil liberties); and items 9–12 are indicators of F_3 (international relations). The lack of arrows connecting the F's represents the fact that we are for the time being assuming that these factors are completely uncorrelated. The basic assumption behind this kind of model is that the underlying attitudes or mental states actually cause the individual to respond in given ways to the items 1–12. Of course there will be other factors that also affect each response, but we assume that whatever these may be, they do not affect the *patterning* of responses. Put another way, we may conceive of the responses to each question as having been caused by one of the three factors, plus a number of variables that are uniquely related to that single item.

If these assumptions were in fact correct, we would anticipate that items 1–4 would be intercorrelated with each other due to the common influence of F_1. In terms of the discussion of the previous chapter, we would say that they would be spuriously related due to their common cause (here, economic conservatism). If F_1 could be directly measured and controlled, the intercorrelations among these four items should reduce to zero, since their remaining causes would have nothing in common. The same should apply to the item sets 5–8 and 9–12.

But if we were to examine the relationships *between* item sets, we would expect to find all intercorrelations to be approximately zero. That is, item 1 should not be related to items 5–12, and so forth. Knowing how a person responded to a question dealing with economic policy (say, endorsement of social security) should not help us whatsoever in predicting how he will respond to any of the civil liberties or international relations questions. Thus in this very simple kind of situation we would expect to find three sets of four indicators each, with correlations within sets being reasonably high but with very low correlations between sets. If such simple results were actually found, we might infer that the twelve questions were tapping three unrelated factors, and by looking carefully at the wording of the questions in each set, we might infer the underlying factors.

Unfortunately, we seldom get such simple and clear-cut results. It is much more likely that some interrelationships among items will be strong, others will be moderate, and still others approximately zero. Thus we will require adequate measures of the strength of these interrelationships plus a much more rigorous procedure for inferring the underlying factors. Such measures and procedures exist, but the subject is far too technical to be discussed in the present context. However, it is possible to indicate two kinds of complications that may arise in order to suggest the kinds of approaches that can be used.

One of these possibilities is diagramed in Figure 7 and the second in Figure 8. Obviously the two kinds of situations can be combined, and it is possible that there will be many more than three factors operative. In Figure 7 the three factors are themselves interrelated, as indicated by the curved arrows connecting them. For example, we would ordinarily predict that people who are economic liberals are also liberal with respect to civil liberties and international relations. If so, then we would expect to find correlations among all pairs of questions, although in most cases the correlations within any given set should be

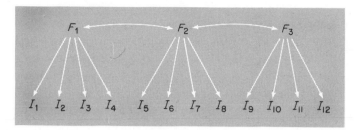

Figure 7

stronger than those between sets. That is, item 1 should be more highly related (or predictive) to items 2–4 than to the remaining items. If this kind of pattern prevails consistently, then we might infer that the model of Figure 7 is the correct one.

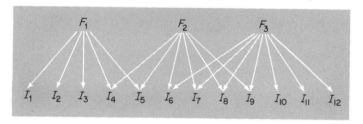

Figure 8

But it is also possible that a single item will tap more than one factor, as illustrated in Figure 8. A question may be double-barreled, tapping both civil liberties and international relations (e.g., "All members of the Communist Party should be either jailed or exported"). Suppose that item 4 tapped both F_1 and F_2. Then this particular item should be correlated with sets 1–3 and 5–8, though perhaps it might be less highly related to any of them than would be expected if it clearly belonged to one set or the other.

In more complex examples such as these, a simple inspection of the correlations among items will not be sufficient to enable one to infer the underlying factors. What is needed are quantitative techniques that make it possible to estimate the degree to which each item is measuring each factor, as well as the number of such factors and their interrelationships. It turns out that although such techniques exist and have been well studied under the label of "factor analysis," there are in effect too many unknowns in the theoretical system to give unique estimates of the factors without further assumptions. It again becomes necessary to supplement the empirical analysis with theoretical assumptions, many of which will be inherently untestable and some of which will be more plausible than others. Once more, the hypercritical skeptic can always question these assumptions. The careful social scientist will always caution his reader that these assumptions are being made, so that the more reasonable skeptic can make constructive suggestions for improving the research.

GUTTMAN SCALING

Before leaving the subject of attitude measurement, let us consider one other kind of procedure for inferring dimensionality that is particularly useful where the objective is to reduce the number of items to a relatively small number that tap a single dimension. This procedure is referred to as Guttman Scaling and is based on a very simple principle and definition of a cumulative (ordinal) scale. The basic idea is that if individuals can be properly ranked along a single continuum or dimension, then if A is greater than B, he should possess all of the attributes of B plus at least one more. In terms of attitudinal questions, if A is more conservative than B, then he should endorse all of the conservative items that B has endorsed plus at least one more.

This principle can be illustrated in terms of an arithmetic test consisting of items that get more and more difficult. Suppose there are five such items. Presumably a person who misses only one question should solve the first four easier questions and miss the last. Someone who misses two questions should solve the first three correctly and miss the last two. If this pattern prevails perfectly, then it will be possible to tell exactly which questions a person missed if we know his total score. This criterion does not allow for careless mistakes or "errors." No one is supposed to miss the first question and get the others correct.

In terms of our prejudice example, it has been found empirically that what sociologists call "social distance" items often form this kind of cumulative scale with very few "errors." At the one extreme can be placed an item involving a personal commitment to intermarriage, such as "Would you be willing to marry a black person?" Somewhat less extreme would be a question tapping one's willingness to associate intimately with blacks as social equals, such as "Would you be willing to have a black person in your home as an overnight guest?" At the opposite extreme would be a question such as "Would you be willing to shop at a store where there are black customers?" Presumably any white who is willing to marry a black person would be willing to have a black as an overnight guest, and a white who would be willing to have the black person as a guest would be willing to shop near one. But a white person who is willing to have a black overnight guest may not be willing to marry a black.

If the five items formed a perfect scale, then they could be arranged in order according to degree of favorableness implied. If each item involved a yes-no response (to simplify the example), the results might be as follows:

Persons	Items									
	1 Yes	2 Yes	3 Yes	4 Yes	5 Yes	1 No	2 No	3 No	4 No	5 No
type 1	X	X	X	X	X					
	X	X	X	X	X					
type 2		X	X	X	X	X				
		X	X	X	X	X				
		X	X	X	X	X				
type 3			X	X	X	X	X			
			X	X	X	X	X			
type 4				X	X	X	X	X		
type 5					X	X	X	X	X	
					X	X	X	X	X	
type 6						X	X	X	X	X
						X	X	X	X	X

In the case of a perfect scale, there will be a diagonal pattern of X's and exactly one more type of response pattern than there are questions (with yes-no answers). In this example there are two persons who answered "yes" to all five questions. Three answered "no" to the first question (say, dealing with marriage) but "yes" to all of the remaining four questions. Two persons failed to endorse the first two questions but answered "yes" to the remaining three, and so forth. Notice that there are no peculiar or idiosyncratic answers, such as that of answering "no" only to the fourth question. Of course, with real data we will never obtain such clear-cut results. There will always be "errors," which will show up as X's in peculiar, off-diagonal locations.

The problem is how to deal with such "errors." If there are very few off-diagonal X's, and if they appear to be randomly scattered, then perhaps they can be considered as true errors or as idiosyncratic responses due to peculiar experiences of the respondents. But what if there were as many as 20 per cent "errors"? And suppose most of these involved interchanges between questions 2 and 3. How do we know they are true errors? In fact, we would probably feel rather foolish if we were to confront a white respondent and tell him he had been "in error" (or inconsistent) if he had indicated that he would be willing to have a black boss but not a black neighbor. Just because most whites might be more willing to have a black neighbor than a black boss, does this mean that this particular respondent is in some sense in error or irrational?

This problem seems to reduce to whether or not the investigator wishes to *assume* that there is a single underlying dimension and that departures from a perfect scale are to be considered as response errors, or whether he is willing to admit a greater degree of complexity. For example, it is entirely possible that the items are tapping two distinct dimensions and that items 2 and 3 stand in different relationships to each other on these two dimensions. If item 2 represents a higher degree of prejudice on the first dimension, but item 3 represents a higher degree on the second, then some individuals will answer "yes" to question 2 and "no" to question 3, whereas others will reverse the pattern. The existence of large numbers of *patterned* errors therefore suggests the possibility that more than one dimension is being tapped. Again it becomes necessary to develop reasonably technical criteria for deciding which alternative explanation to accept, and once more the skeptic may choose to elect whichever explanation the investigator rejects. It is therefore essential that both be well aware of the criteria that are being used, as well as the mathematical properties of the scaling procedures.

This brief discussion of attitude measurement should be sufficient to indicate some of the complexities involved and the necessity for careful quantitative work. I hope it also conveys the impression that a good deal has already been accomplished, but that a great deal more needs to be done.

Measurement of Group Properties

The field of attitude measurement illustrates very well many of the problems of indirect measurement, and techniques such as factor analysis and Guttman scaling can be applied in a number of areas in addition to attitude measurement. But there are many other kinds of measurement problems faced by social scientists, only some of which can be discussed in this brief overview of the field. While psychologists deal almost exclusively with generalizations about individuals (animals as well as human beings), the remaining social sciences are often more concerned with propositions about groups of one kind or another. These range from small cliques and families to entire societies. Nevertheless, much of our data comes to us in the form of measures on individuals or small groupings, thus raising the problem of developing ways of aggregating these individual measures so as to construct measures that are appropriate to the entire group.

There have been numerous philosophical debates over the question of whether persons are more "real" than groups. The extreme nominalist position is that groups are simple aggregates of individuals, that they possess a "reality" only in the minds of social scientists, and that there is little to be gained from studying these groups as distinct entities. The realist position, by contrast, stresses the argument that groups have existences quite apart from those of their individual members, though of course they cannot be touched and would go out of existence if all of their members were to disappear. Much of this debate seems to turn on rather ambiguous questions concerning what one means by the statement that groups "exist." There is no need, here, to enter into such a debate except to point out that, quite apart from questions of the reality of groups, it is often *useful* to make statements about groups and to measure group properties of a very different kind from properties that can be associated with single individuals.

A few examples should make this point obvious. Political scientists speak about the behavior of nations, and they analyze competition among nations in much the same way as a psychologist might analyze competition among children. In discussing nations or societies it is useful to characterize them in terms of such factors as their size, their forms of government, their homogeneity with respect to various characteristics, their religious systems, their gross national products, and so forth. One may then state theoretical propositions relating size to concentration of political power, the nature of economic systems to political systems, and so forth, and data may be collected and analyzed in much the same way as is done in the case of persons. The number of "cases" becomes the number of nations, but otherwise the basic principles and strategies of analysis are the same. But the practical problems are in many respects more difficult.

Foremost among these practical problems is that of the very great expenditures of time and money that are necessary in the data collection process. It is expensive enough to conduct a careful survey of two thousand persons in a single city. But if comparable data were to be collected on persons in as many as two hundred cities, the cost would seem prohibitive. Most social research is conducted by single individuals or small research teams with very limited budgets, and therefore comparative work on large numbers of large-scale units such as communities or societies is practically always confined to what are referred to as "secondary analyses" of data that have been collected for other purposes. In some cases, these data are excellent and well standardized from one community to another. Such is the case with respect to the U.S. Census and other censuses in modern westernized societies. Censuses conducted in so-called underdeveloped countries, however, are practically always of poor quality and often biased in unknown ways.

Whenever the social scientist wishes to deal with groups as large as entire societies, it becomes extremely difficult to obtain truly comparable data. Even where there are high-quality data in each nation, the definitions used in collecting and classifying these data are often very different from one country to the next. In one country the definition of an "urban" area may be any community of five thousand or more population; in a second it may be one of ten thousand or more; and in a third it may be set at the two thousand level. Countries are divided into very different types of smaller units (e.g., states, cantons, provinces), each of which may have its own policies with respect to the collection of data. Even within a single country, policies of local units may vary considerably. For example, crime statistics in the United States are notoriously poor and underestimate actual crime rates by unknown degrees. Some kinds of crimes, such as homicides, are much more likely to come to the attention of the authorities than are others, such as rape or petty theft, and official crime rates are very likely to reflect differential reporting by the public and differential efficiencies of the police.

Whenever a social scientist is forced to use secondary sources for his data, he practically always must settle for measures other than those he would really like to obtain. In many instances the information will not be available because the collecting agency had a policy against collecting it (e.g., religion in the case of the U.S. Census) or (more likely) because it never occurred to them to collect it. Obviously, a census is a very expensive operation, as is a public opinion poll, and only a small fraction of the potentially useful questions can be asked. And, of course, a given respondent cannot be asked too many questions, since it has generally been found that approximately one hour of interviewing time is optimal in terms of keeping refusal rates at a reasonable level.

We are back to discussing individual respondents, whereas the focus of this section is supposedly on groups as units of analysis. This raises a second major problem of measurement in the case of these larger units, one which has yet to receive the careful attention of most social scientists except possibly for economists. Many of the measures or variables appropriate to groups must be obtained by aggregating scores for persons. A very trivial case is that of the size of the group, which is obtained by simply counting all its members. There are many other kinds of aggregate measures that can be similarly obtained, namely those that involve percentages of the members who belong in various categories. Thus cities (or counties) can be characterized in terms of variables such as per cent non-white, per cent of the labor force that is unemployed or white-collar, or by measures of what is typical, such as median income, mean years of schooling, or average age of its dwelling units. More complex derived measures can also be constructed. For example, by counting the relative numbers of whites and non-whites in all city blocks, a measure of residential segregation can be computed for each city.

Much more difficult problems of aggregation arise in instances where persons should not all receive the same weights but where exact criteria for weighting cannot be easily developed. Suppose one wanted to obtain a measure indicating the average "climate" of prejudice in each of one hundred communities. Obviously some people should be given more weight than others, since they will not all be equally influential. But how does one decide how much weight to give the mayor, the newspaper editor, top management, and so forth? This depends on an accurate measure of influence, which would be extremely expensive to obtain. Furthermore, the weights assigned to each individual would have to differ according to each issue area being studied. Someone with considerable impact on racial attitudes might have very little influence on economic issues. And unless at least an interval-scale level of measurement can be attained for the measures of individual attitudes, their separate scores cannot be legitimately "added" or averaged. Many of these rather subtle problems of forming aggregate measures have not yet been well studied, since few social scientists have had the necessary resources to collect adequate data in the first place. But sooner or later they must be resolved if measurement is to be improved.

A third kind of difficulty stems from the fact that groups often have rather fuzzy boundaries or boundaries that have been arbitrarily defined for political or other kinds of practical reasons. There can be no doubt where John Jones ends and Bill Brown begins, and therefore persons may be counted and sorted into mutually exclusive and exhaustive categories. But exactly what are the boundaries of the Chicago metropolitan area or Mary Smith's sewing circle? Most informal cliques have members that come and go. Although churches and other voluntary organizations may have membership lists, we all know that many persons so listed are not really members in any sociological sense. While it might appear to outsiders that such lists are merely being padded, those responsible for constructing the lists are well aware of the ambiguities involved. Some people drop out without telling anyone, or they pretend to themselves that they are still members. Many groups are such that their memberships shade into each other imperceptibly. This is often true of adjacent communities, but it is also the case with respect to most informal cliques. Club women may engage in endless discussions about whether Susan Snodgrass is really "in" with a certain crowd, but this merely reflects the same kind of problem with which social scientists must learn to deal more rigorously.

This problem of fuzziness of group boundaries has been especially troublesome to anthropologists studying so-called primitive peoples. Unlike the nation state, a primitive "society" may be very loosely defined. Is it a single community? A group of several bound together by political means? Or a clustering of communities linked by a common language or economy? Different investigators may reach different conclusions, depending on the criteria they prefer. I do not wish to leave the impression that *no* adequate guidelines can be found, but we have here an example of a methodological problem that does not exist as long as one's attention is confined to persons or to readily distinguishable units of any kind.

Closely related to this problem of group boundaries is that of mutual influence across these rather ill-defined boundaries. Suppose, for example, that an anthropologist wants to study the influence of economic systems on political development. He may divide Black Africa into one hundred societies, whereas a second anthropologist might have distinguished only twenty-nine societies. Obviously the first anthropologist is using smaller units, which gives him the advantage of having more cases for statistical purposes. But suppose many of his societies are so closely interconnected that many of them merely borrow ideas from the others (as also occurs in the case of all other kinds of social groupings). Both anthropologists may be theoretically interested in the causal processes that produce a practical connection between economic and political systems. They would be on solid ground if they could assume that each observation (i.e., each society) constituted an independent replication, in the same sense that each flip of a coin is independent of the others or each replication of an experiment is independent of all others.[2]

The problem with adjacent societies, and with adjacent people for that matter, is that they tend to influence each other in ways that may distort our inferences about the true causal processes. If one society has a complex division of labor and a complex political system, and if its neighbor is just like it, it is difficult to tell to what degree each developed autonomously and to what degree they should really be treated as one and the same society. This particular kind of problem can only be analyzed by complex statistical procedures and

[2] This notion of independence can be pinned down by saying that if two events are independent, then knowing the outcome of one does not help us predict the outcome of the other. Knowing that an honest coin has come up heads on the first flip does not help us predict what will happen on the next flip.

is closely parallel to problems faced by economists who take repeated measures on the same units (say, business firms) over a large number of points in time. Factors affecting the outcomes at time 1 may be highly related to factors affecting them at times 2 and 3, and we again encounter a case in which repeated observations are not independent.

In general it is usually found that the smaller the time intervals, and the smaller the group units, the more serious this particular difficulty becomes. In effect, this places limits on the number of pieces into which the pie can be sliced. If a social scientist really believed that one sized unit was as good as another, he would simply use a very large number of small units (e.g., counties instead of states), thereby either increasing the size of his sample or cutting down the amount of his work. But as we have generally seen to be the case, life just isn't that simple. At each decision point there will be pro's and con's to consider, and it is often unfortunately true that such decisions must be made on the basis of enlightened guesses rather than solid fact. But as a science matures, the relative proportion of guesses is gradually reduced.

6

Some Implications

In this very short book I have tried to convey some understanding of the complexities that are encountered in social research, without going into any of the technical details. There are several impressions I wish to leave. The first is that research is a technical business that requires prolonged training and experience, though of course some kinds of research are much more complex than others. The second is that progress is being made in terms of our basic understanding of this research process, but many of the difficulties social scientists encounter stem from the sheer scale of the research that would be necessary in order to obtain definitive results.

Finally, I have tried to emphasize that in most practical situations of interest to the student and layman, the social scientist can provide only tentative answers. In part this is due to inherent limitations of the scientific method and to the fact that only a handful of the variables that may be operative can be studied at one time. But it is also due to the immaturity of the social sciences and to limitations of time and money. There are simply too few social scientists and too few resources to study every problem in which someone might be interested.

Given the problems we face in getting beyond the purely exploratory study, it seems to me that social research must become much more ambitious in scope. This is particularly the case where cross-cultural comparisons are being made and where it is necessary to study the simultaneous operation of large numbers of variables. Sample surveys must be larger and better coordinated, so that comparable data can be accumulated. Comparisons of different communities and nations have been notably handicapped by lack of data standardization, and the individual investigator can hardly be expected to overcome this difficulty. Instead, the basic data must be collected by large-scale research organizations and made available to individual analysts at minimal cost. It is in the collection of these data that the major costs of research are encountered. This problem will increase in magnitude if we take seriously the need for longitudinal data collected at regular time intervals.

A question closely related to that of the scale of social science research is that of the scope of its coverage. Put succinctly, the dilemma is one of whether we should devote our major energies to exploring a wider and wider range of social phenomena or whether we should study a much smaller number in greater depth. With very limited financing and small-scale projects, the tendency is to spread out to cover a wide variety of subjects. This orientation can also be justified on the grounds that it is at present premature to devote our energies to a few topics, not knowing which ones will ultimately turn out to be the most fruitful ones from the standpoint of the development of scientific knowledge.

Nevertheless, it seems to me that we may be spreading ourselves too thin. A casual glance at the list of specialties within sociology indicates that special areas and subareas have been proliferating at a rapid pace. There is now a "sociology of X" for just about every social phenomenon X that exists, even a "sociology of pets"! Even with a modest growth in sociological manpower, this increasing scope of the field must come at the expense of depth in a few. It seems to me that such diversification is one reason why there has not been sufficient attention given to the careful measurement and conceptualization of variables and to the need for replication studies of the kind that are commonly found in the physical sciences. Replications are expensive, but they are also not rewarded. A graduate student is encouraged to be "original" and "creative," which usually means that he is rewarded more for finding a new and interesting topic or theoretical perspective than for studying in depth something that has already been investigated.

Another reason why social scientists, particularly sociologists, seem to be spreading themselves so thin is that they have been highly responsive to the demands for applied research. In some cases, this has meant doing research in areas where money can be found. In many others, it results from a social conscience and a desire to work on problems that are of immediate practical concern. This is all to the common good, since many useful theoretical and methodological insights have come from the study of social problems and since many new recruits are attracted to the social sciences because of their interest in one or another social problem.

The difficulty seems to lie in the on-and-off policies of sponsoring agencies with respect to social problem areas. As indicated in the introductory chapter, social scientists until recently have found it extremely difficult to obtain financing in the field of minority-group relations, owing to its controversial nature. At the present time financial support in this area is more than adequate, as long as the study deals with lower-class blacks, poverty, or crime and violence. Under other political conditions, however, these sources of support may very well be dried up.

This tendency for research to flow in the direction dictated by federal funds is even more common in the physical sciences, where billions are being spent on rocket research and electronics, with obvious military overtones. In a democratic society, this ability of a few governmental agencies to direct the funding of research is not only potentially dangerous. It also may inhibit the healthy development of basic research, which is not oriented to producing results of immediate practical utility. Only an enlightened governmental policy can prevent or inhibit this tendency, and for this reason it is essential that the granting agencies be placed beyond the close supervision of politicians. There is a kind of safety in numbers here, in that a plurality of granting agencies, each under the direction of different sets of social scientists, should provide greater insurance against a one-sided development.

A closely related difficulty in relation to the financing of research has been the tendency of granting agencies to prefer short-run projects that can show immediate payoffs. The idea of a longitudinal study conducted over a period of perhaps twenty years is appealing to social scientists but much less so to persons who are held accountable for specific results. Obviously, long-range studies cannot be planned and adequately financed if they are subject to changes in policy according to the political party that happens to be in office.

Yet applied research must be carried out, though not to the exclusion of basic research (if, indeed, applied and basic research represent opposites on a single continuum). Certain kinds of applied research would not seem to require more than a year or two of training beyond the A.B. degree. In particular, many studies are designed to ascertain certain facts, upon which intelligent policies are to be based. How many citizens are in favor of increased social security payments? What is the demand for low-cost housing in a particular area? Do whites really oppose school integration? These kinds of questions can be answered by means of public opinion polls and can be analyzed by persons with a few semesters' training in applied statistics and research methods courses. Perhaps there should be specialized centers where such training can be obtained along with practical experience in the construction of questionnaires, sampling, and other survey methodology.[1]

---

[1] If there were a regular market for persons with an A.B. degree trained in social science research, this might justify a special type of undergraduate major with a heavy emphasis on such topics as applied statistics, sampling theory and practice, computer applications, questionnaire construction, and so forth.

There are other kinds of applied research that require much more training. In particular, there is a great need for evaluation research of ongoing pilot projects. Such evaluation research requires the assessment of the effects of the program under study, with careful attention to controls for extraneous factors and a knowledge of the principles of experimental design. Evaluation research is all the more useful if the investigator can apply social science principles to his research findings in order to make specific recommendations as to how the program could be improved. Ideally, these recommendations could be put into effect, the results again evaluated, and new theoretical and practical insights gained in the process. Obviously, this kind of applied research requires considerable training and experience on the part of the investigator.

Social scientists differ widely in their views about applied research, though most would undoubtedly endorse the notion that there must be a healthy balance between basic and applied research. But since no single piece of research can be simply classed as being entirely applied or unapplied, these differences of opinion will probably not lead to serious difficulties in the near future. I assume, however, that there is a high degree of consensus among all social scientists that the better their work is understood among the general citizenry, the more likely it is that the social sciences will be permitted and encouraged to develop more rapidly toward maturity.

Index